# WHAT DOES REVELATION REVEAL?

## UNLOCKING THE MYSTERY

Warren Carter

Abingdon Press
Nashville

WHAT DOES REVELATION REVEAL?
UNLOCKING THE MYSTERY

*Copyright © 2011 by Abingdon Press*

*This book is printed on acid-free paper.*

**Library of Congress Cataloging-in-Publication Data**

Carter, Warren, 1955-
   What does Revelation reveal? : unlocking the mystery / Warren Carter.
     p.   cm.
   ISBN 978-1-4267-1014-8 (pbk. : alk. paper)
   1. Bible. N.T. Revelation—Textbooks.   I. Title.
   BS2825.55.C37 2011
   228'.06—dc23
                                                              2011018046

Map on page 10 is adapted from The Common English Bible © 2010 Common English Bible.

11 12 13 14 15 16 17 18 19 20—10 9 8 7 6 5 4 3 2 1

MANUFACTURED IN THE UNITED STATES OF AMERICA

# Contents

# Preface

R evelation is a tricky book to read. How do we read it? What is it about? And does it have anything to say to contemporary Christians who are not interested in the rapture? This book addresses these three issues.

It begins by thinking about reading strategies for the book of Revelation (ch. 1). It then engages the contents of Revelation by asking the question, "What *does* Revelation reveal?" Dividing Revelation into eight sections, it identifies eight "revelations." The last chapter explores some possible implications of Revelation's revelations for contemporary readers.

This book invites readers of Revelation to think about how and what they are reading. Revelation needs our thoughtful and careful engagement so that we might discern ways in which we might appropriately respond to it.

This book is written for Bible study groups and for seminary and college courses on Revelation. Bible study groups could read the chapters of Revelation and the corresponding chapter in this book ahead of time, and talk about their insights and reflections in their time together. Questions at the end of each chapter may assist that conversation.

# CHAPTER 1

# Leaving Revelation Behind?

Revelation has often been a controversial book. Throughout the church's two thousand-year history, it has been "read" in all sorts of ways. It has frequently been used as a weapon against opponents. It has been used to "scare the hell out of people and people out of hell." Some select groups have claimed to possess the key to its right interpretation, which the rest of us lack.

By the same token, some have found its descriptions of heavenly worship very moving. At various times and places in the church's long history when governments or groups tried to forbid worship and service for God, some have found its demand for loyalty, even to death in martyrdom, to be sustaining and motivating. Some have found its vision of a world in which all things are finally in right relationship with God an inspiration to lives invested in a quest for justice in the present world.

Then there are some people who just can't get enough of the book of Revelation. They read it constantly. They're always going to Bible studies and conferences to hear speakers update the latest revelation on Revelation. They talk about being "premillenialists," about the "tribulation," about "the rapture." They see connections between reports on their favorite news channels and some verse somewhere in Revelation. Everything is a "sign of the times." Everything is part of the countdown till the world is destroyed and Jesus returns, whether in the year 1988, or 2000, or 2012 or.... They know they won't be left behind.

On the other hand, some folks don't want anything to do with Revelation. They find it scary or weird, the obsession with it freaky, and think it simply irrelevant to any news report. Despite its claim to be a revelation, they find it obscure and frustratingly concealing. They often attend churches where there is little preaching from or reference to Revelation and they like it that way. They don't understand or care about terms like "premillenialists," "tribulation," or "rapture." They often think those who take Revelation really seriously are fanatics at best and crazy at worst. They find the very notion of the end of the world or that some will be "left behind" distasteful and intolerant. In fact, they're quite happy to have Revelation left behind.

These very different evaluations of and approaches to Revelation raise a central question. How do we read this difficult book? I am using the word *read* to mean "how we make meaning or sense of Revelation." How do we understand it? What reading strategies or approaches are helpful and which are unhelpful for making meaning of this book? *How* we read the book of Revelation very much determines what meaning we make of it. That means it is worth thinking carefully about the reading strategies that can be used for the book.

In this chapter I will evaluate two quite different ways of reading Revelation. With each approach I will show the decisions that each makes about how to read Revelation. Both strategies have strengths and weaknesses. From our discussion will emerge a third strategy that I suggest offers a more adequate approach. In the subsequent chapters I will use this third strategy to "make meaning" of Revelation by asking the central question: what does Revelation reveal? Remember, the reading strategies we adopt very much shape the meaning we will make as we read Revelation.

## Reading Strategy 1

This approach should really be called a "nonreading strategy." Some people think Revelation is best left unread. Why?

First, some find Revelation a strange book with weird creatures, bizarre numbers, and strange sequences of visions. It doesn't seem to make sense. It's too fanciful and bizarre.

Second, some find Revelation to be an offensive book. It seems to be full of visions of destruction. God appears angry and vengeful. It has unkind things to say about Jews. It presents women in negative ways. Others find it smug and self-righteous, dangerous in its declarations of favor for Jesus-believers and destructive for everyone who does not believe.

Third, some are turned off from Revelation by all the interpretations that have been offered for the book. Numerous interpretations have turned out to be wrong because what they claimed Revelation to be predicting did not happen. As the world approached the year 1000 C.E., there were numerous readings of Revelation that predicted the end of the world. Similar things happened as the world approached the year 2000 (remember Y2K?) and are happening now as we approach 2012 (based on Mayan predictions). Such readings seem so arbitrary—and obviously off target.

One conclusion to draw from such observations is that we need not bother with Revelation. But if Revelation can be read in such obviously wrong and offensive ways, we surely need to be thinking carefully about how we read it and the meaning we make from it. Is it offensive? Is it dangerous? Is its interpretation arbitrary? Does it predict the future? These are important questions to engage, especially so when Revelation belongs to the Scriptures of the church. The community of faith is an important location to think about, talk about, and evaluate such issues.

# Reading Strategy 2

The most popular way of reading Revelation today understands it as a book that predicts the end of the world that will soon take place.

This approach, known as a dispensationalist or premillenialist approach, has been popularized by several best-selling books and movies. Published in 1970, Hal Lindsey's book *The Late Great Planet Earth* interprets Revelation and some other biblical books (especially Ezekiel and Daniel) in relation to current events of the 1970s and 1980s. Lindsey sees these decades up to 1988—forty years or a generation after the establishment of the state of Israel—as especially important in leading up to the end of the world. Before then, at least three things will happen: (1) Believers will be raptured (taken up to heaven), (2) Jesus will return before the time of the seven-year tribulation, and (3) Jesus will establish his thousand-year reign. Lindsey's emphasis on 1988 as the decisive year for accomplishing God's purposes turned out to be wrong. I bought Lindsey's book in the early 1980s and since 1989 I have been waiting for a refund.

Between 1995 and 2007, the Left Behind series of sixteen best-selling novels written by Tim LaHaye and Jerry B. Jenkins appeared. There were also teen versions, movies, dramatizations for radio, and video games. The technique of using novels (and films) to dramatize events that this reading strategy understands Revelation to be predicting is not a new approach. There are examples of similar novels from the early twentieth century.

The Left Behind novels focus on the time after God has "raptured" believers before Jesus returns to establish his thousand-year reign. Those who are "left behind," the focus of the series, live in a world that is under the sway of the secretary-general of the United Nations, Nicolae Jetty Carpathia. For those in the know, he is the Antichrist who opposes God's purposes. A small group of believers emerges who understand that the end of the world is very near. They seek to save people in preparation for the coming time of tribulation in which God will judge the world.

These are but a couple of examples of this very popular reading strategy. What assumptions are at work in this reading strategy? What decisions about how to read Revelation does this approach make?

**Five Assumptions**

1. This reading strategy understands Revelation as a book of future predictions. This understanding comes from Revelation's description of itself as a "prophecy" (1:3; 22:7). The term "prophecy" is understood in this strategy to mean that Revelation foretells events that will very soon take place to restore the world in line with God's will.

2. This reading strategy reads Revelation as referring to literal events that will soon take place. It does not understand Revelation's language to be symbolic or poetic. So when Rev 11:2 depicts "the nations" trampling over Jerusalem for "forty-two months" (three and a half years), this is understood to be a literal event. Likewise, the 144,000 will literally be gathered on Mount Zion (14:1), a final battle will occur at Megiddo in north Israel (Armageddon; 16:12-16), Christ will establish a thousand-year reign (20:4-6), there will be a literal New Jerusalem (21:9-27). Those who employ this approach pay close attention to contemporary events to identify these biblical events beginning to take place.

3. This reading strategy chooses to focus on our contemporary world. It understands that Revelation has not made sense to any previous generations. But now, this reading strategy claims, it makes sense to us because we stand on the edge of what Revelation is predicting will take place any day now. It understands that Revelation depicts the present world as out-of-shape and under God's judgment. Things are so bad that humans cannot do anything about them. It sees Revelation predicting future events through which God will very soon intervene to rescue the world.

4. This reading strategy for Revelation is eclectic. It chooses to interpret Revelation by drawing on other New Testament writings. So it includes the ideas of a rapture (God's removal of believers from the earth) and of the Antichrist. Neither of these elements appears in Revelation. The first is borrowed from Paul in 1 Thess 4:17. The second is borrowed from 1 and 2 John.

5. Finally, this reading strategy elicits a largely passive response from readers. Its emphasis on the world being so out-of-shape means that God's imminent intervention is the only available remedy. Humans shouldn't and can't do anything about the present state of the world. Readers are to remain watchful and faithful in awaiting God's intervention, while warning others about being prepared for what is soon to happen and how not to be left behind.

## Assessing Reading Strategy 2

This reading strategy has some important strengths. It is a popular reading strategy because it takes seriously human fears and anxieties about the world and offers the hope of God's imminent intervention. It makes sense of the present by putting it in the context of God's good purposes. It assures people about the future by predicting events that will very soon enact those purposes. It takes Revelation as a biblical document seriously and shows how it can be relevant to people's lives.

But while these are significant strengths, this strategy has some serious weaknesses. One is the assumption that Revelation predicts events that will come to pass only in our time. This claim means that only present-day readers can make sense of Revelation. The implication of this approach is that the writer of Revelation did not know what he was writing and that Revelation, though written two thousand years ago, has not been comprehensible since to any readers across the last two millennia. These claims are simply not convincing. Human beings, even writers of Scripture, are not robots. And communities of believers have always made meaning of the writings in the canon for their own lives.

A second weakness is that this approach, focused on predicting future events, takes no account of the circumstances from which this text originated and that which it addressed. The strategy deems these past circumstances to be irrelevant. Only the present (twenty-first century) and future matter. Such a view fails to take seriously that God is involved in human history and events in the past, as well as the present and imminent future.

A third weakness concerns understanding Revelation as a prophecy that predicts future events. While Revelation identifies itself as a prophecy (1:3), we need to ask what this word *prophecy* means. In strategy 2, the word often means to predict or foretell the future. But across the biblical tradition, the word *prophecy* often has a different meaning.

While prophets *can* predict future events, prophets in the Bible are predominantly concerned with the present. They analyze or interpret present situations in relation to God's purposes (Isa 5:1-7). They denounce injustice and the misuse of power (Isa 1:17, 28). They interpret international events from God's perspectives (Isa 7-8, 10). They declare God's will and what God requires (Jer 2:11-25). When they talk of the future, they often do so in terms of the consequences of the present (Isa 35).

6

That is, prophets preach more than they predict. They proclaim a word of the Lord to the present circumstances of their audience more than they forecast the future. Prophets "forth-tell" more than they foretell. Prophets analyze and interpret the present in terms of God's purposes rather than declare tomorrow's headlines today. A reading strategy that concentrates on prophecy as predicting the future significantly misreads Revelation by trying to make it do what it cannot do.

Moreover, Revelation does not consist of only one genre or type of literature. It also employs two other genres, that of a "revelation" or an "apocalypse" (1:1), and a letter (1:4; chs. 2–3). I will explain these genres in the next chapter, but it is sufficient to note here that both apocalypses and letters also address the present circumstances of their readers. Reading strategy 2 ignores these genres and their focus on the present.

The recognition of these multiple genres raises questions about the literal understanding of Revelation's language that this reading strategy employs. Prophecies and apocalypses often use symbolic or metaphorical language to talk about God's ways and to describe social conditions. This poetic language engages our imagination, it creates an overall impression, it establishes a general effect. Details contribute to this larger impression; they are not meant to be interpreted literally.

To confuse symbolic language as literal language leads to serious misunderstanding. If someone says, "Give me a hand," we recognize immediately that this is a metaphor, that the person wants our help. We don't literally cut off a hand and give it to the person. Understanding Revelation's symbolic language—which often draws on the language of the Hebrew Bible as well as first-century culture—is a significant challenge in reading Revelation.

Further, as we noted above, reading strategy 2 borrows several notions such as "the rapture" and "Antichrist" from other New Testament writings to interpret Revelation. The problem is, though, that Revelation does not refer to a rapture. It does not provide the option of believers miraculously escaping the world and its tribulation by being taken up into heaven. In fact, Revelation 21 reverses any such notion and has the New Jerusalem and God's presence coming down from heaven to be among people on earth! Nor does Revelation use the term *Antichrist*. This reading strategy randomly imports these notions from other New Testament writings. The text of 1 and 2 John refers to opponents in a church fight as "antichrists" (plural, not the singular "Antichrist") and not as some international figure or world ruler. Those who use this strategy have often employed this notion of the Antichrist in negative and selective ways to vilify various social and political figures with whom they disagree. Importing such notions into the interpretation of Revelation distorts its meaning.

And finally, this reading strategy fundamentally creates passive readers who remain indifferent to the pain and brokenness of the world while they wait for God's intervention. Such indifference or escape is contrary to Revelation's own teaching, as well as to that of the biblical tradition. God's people are to be in partnership with God, agents of God's healing and life-giving work in the world, not disengaged from our brokenness and escapees from the world. A reading strategy that creates readers so out of step with the biblical message needs an alternative.

# Reading Strategy 3

From this evaluation of the second reading strategy, a third strategy for reading Revelation emerges. It has four dimensions. I will mention them here briefly and elaborate them in the next few chapters.

## 1. Circumstances Addressed

This strategy recognizes that Revelation is an ancient text. It comes from a time and culture vastly different from our own (see appendix A for discussion). Some two thousand years and many cultural changes separate us from it. This ancient world has left its mark on Revelation in its language and forms of thought, just as our world influences us as readers. We know that cultures and the meaning of words change over time. The word *peculiar*, for example, once meant "special"; now it means "weird." The word *gay* once meant "happy" but now for the most part it designates a same-gender sexual orientation. Recognizing and respecting the time-gap between our world and that of Revelation matters if we are to understand it carefully.

Appropriately, strategy 3 takes seriously the time period when Revelation was written and the circumstances to which it was addressed. Because the writer of Revelation did not have my third-grade teacher, he did not know to put the date on his work. Clues from within Revelation and references to it from other writings suggest it was probably written between 70 and 100 C.E., perhaps in the last decade of the first century. I outline some of the factors leading to this conclusion in appendix A.

And what circumstances did Revelation address? On the basis of the seven letters in chapters 2–3, the writer of Revelation addresses small communities of Christians living in seven cities in the area that we know today as Turkey, but which in the first century was known as the Roman province of Asia. Some interpreters have claimed that these Jesus-believers were persecuted by the Roman Empire because of their faith. But this claim is not supportable. There is no evidence that Rome or the emperor Domitian instigated persecution of Christians in the late first century. There was no law requiring that everybody worship, or offer sacrifice to, the emperor. There is no empire-wide, empire-initiated persecution of Christians until the mid-third century under the emperor Decius. There is some evidence that there were local conflicts between Christians and their neighbors. This might explain the one reference to an actual martyr in Revelation, Antipas (2:13). Most Christians, though, probably lived peaceably in towns and cities throughout the empire.

Other aspects of Revelation point to a division among Jesus-believers rather than to persecution as a key element of the situation that Revelation addresses. The short letters addressed to the seven churches in the Roman province of Asia (modern-day Turkey) in chapters 2–3 discuss various aspects of living as followers of Jesus. One of their central themes concerns how followers of Jesus might conduct themselves in the complex urban world in which they lived. How should they negotiate Roman imperial and cultural power in their cities? Should they think of the empire as a positive force, even one sanctioned by God and doing God's work? Or should they be suspicious of it and keep their distance from its economic greed, social hierarchy, military power, and numerous images and idols that claimed the gods sanctioned its power?

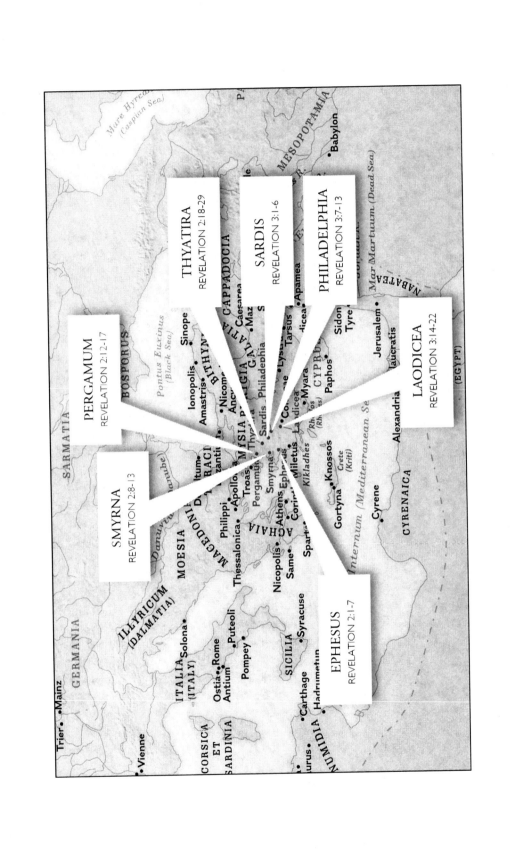

The letters in Revelation 2–3 indicate that there are differing opinions among the believers as to how to answer this question. Some believers are very actively involved in their urban contexts full of temples, idols, and festivals that honor various deities and Roman rulers. The complaint of the author of Revelation is, as we will see, that some believers are *too* culturally accommodated, that they are too much at home in the world, that they are too cozy with the practices and structures of the Roman empire, including the practice of idolatry. He draws a line in the sand. He wants them to establish much more separation and considerable cultural distance.

Revelation seeks to afflict the comfortable, to make those who are culturally accommodated aware that the world in alliance with Roman power is not as God intends it to be. They should withdraw from it, change their ways, and live a countercultural existence that will inevitably bring both opposition or persecution as well as participation in God's coming triumph. I will elaborate this situation in the next two chapters as we discuss the letters in Revelation 2–3.

## 2. Three Genres

In addition to understanding the circumstances from which Revelation emerged and to which it was addressed, this third reading strategy also pays careful attention to the three genres that we identified earlier.

- Revelation is a "revelation" or "apocalypse" (1:1). This form of literature makes a revelation or disclosure about the world and of God's will and purposes for a particular situation. What does Revelation reveal?

- Revelation is also a prophecy (1:3). As we have discussed above, this word denotes in the biblical tradition not primarily a prediction of the future, not a forecasting of what will happen, but a proclamation of God's word to a particular situation. Prophecy is a forth-telling of the divine will, a theological and pastoral interpretation or analysis of the present.

- Revelation is in its overall genre partly a letter (1:4). It also employs seven short letters to each of the seven churches in

11

chapters 2–3. The significance of using a letter form is that it allows specific address to particular circumstances in the present.

This third reading strategy takes seriously the combination of these genres as a means of addressing the conflicts and divisions in the seven churches over how Jesus-believers engage their civic and societal contexts.

## 3. Symbolic Language

This reading strategy understands the language of apocalypses and prophecies like Revelation to be primarily symbolic. Revelation uses imagistic or poetic language. As we will see, this language engages the imagination. It evokes traditions—especially the Hebrew Bible—to construct visions that disclose both the ways of God and the ways of the world. This language works by often evoking literal scenes and realities but then moving beyond them to further meaning and associations. So in 1:10, the writer says, "I heard behind me a loud voice like a trumpet." We imagine, or hear imaginatively, a real voice. But we also hear more. The term "trumpet" evokes a sound associated with getting attention, asserting power and authority, issuing a command, expecting obedience. It is a regal scene that impresses and overawes. Appropriately, in response to hearing a voice like a trumpet, John falls at the speaker's feet (1:17). Being attentive to the multivalent images that Revelation's language stimulates is an important part of this reading strategy.

## 4. Active Response of the Readers

This reading strategy recognizes that readers of Revelation have an active part to play in doing God's purposes on earth. This strategy does not endorse a passive or escapist response. It requires active faithfulness.

## Assessing Reading Strategy 3

This third reading strategy, which we will use through the rest of this book, has numerous strengths. It focuses on the late first-century circumstances from which Revelation emerged and which it addressed. It assumes that Revelation made sense to those who first heard it. It also attends carefully to how Revelation expresses its vision, the multiple genres that it employs, the poetic language that it uses, and the way of life it creates.

There are two significant weaknesses or challenges in this strategy for readers who understand Revelation to be part of the Scriptures of the contemporary church. First, this second strategy is simply not the most common strategy used in contemporary popular readings. Television preachers do not use it. It requires, as we have seen in this chapter, that we do our homework about the late first century, about the book's genres, and about its language and images. It requires a willingness on our part to do some careful study.

And second, while this strategy can very helpfully enable us to understand the past circumstances that shaped Revelation, it can easily lose sight of the present circumstances of contemporary readers. It can lock us, unaware, into the past. It can so focus us on understanding the past that we forget our own situations. We will need to be careful that in attending to its address to these late first-century churches we do not neglect its address to us as present-day believers. Yet attending to its address for contemporary believers, we need to be thoughtful about how we make meaning from this difficult book.

# Study Questions

1. As you begin reading Revelation, what are your initial impressions? Is Revelation hard to understand? Irrelevant? Scary? Intriguing? A book to avoid? Something you've heard about but haven't studied for yourself?

2. This chapter sets out three strategies for reading Revelation. Which approach resonates most with you?

3. In reading chapter 1, have your perceptions about Revelation changed? If so, in what way?

13

CHAPTER 2

# Revelation Reveals That It Is God's Word to God's World (Rev 1)

Dear Reader: Please open your Bible to Revelation 1 and follow each section of that chapter as you read this discussion. Do the same thing through the rest of the chapters of this book.

I have suggested that Revelation addresses a situation of conflict and division among the seven churches in the Roman province of Asia. And there are culture wars within these churches. Jesus-believers do not agree among themselves about how they should engage their civic contexts pervaded by images and symbols of Roman power. Some think active participation is fine. Others, such as the writer of Revelation, want distance and separation from the world.

Revelation's opening chapter is organized in such a way as to claim God's authority for the latter perspective of separation. This is the perspective that the writer "John" supports. Verses 1-3 present Revelation as a revelation and prophecy made known through John as God's authorized spokesperson. Revelation is a prophet-driven writing. In verses 4-8, John frames the material as a letter that he writes to the seven churches. Verses 9-20 elaborate how John came to be commissioned to address the seven churches. The chapter presents a vision in which the risen Jesus authorizes John to write to the churches. That is, it presents Revelation and its

15

author, John, as a writer and prophet authorized by God. John's message to keep their distance from societal participation is presented as God's message. The chapter reveals that it is God's world. The world and the churches are in God's hands.

The interesting thing to observe is how hard the chapter works to underscore John's authority and to establish that he is God's authorized revealer and spokesperson. This emphasis is necessary, precisely because not everyone in the churches who is addressed will agree with this claim. Because of the conflicts and differences among the believers, there are some (many?) in the seven churches who do not recognize John's authority. Some or many do not agree with John's message of separation and societal distance. The presentation of John as authorized and sanctioned by God attempts to undermine the authority and credibility of those in the churches who have different and opposing points of view.

## Revelation as Apocalyptic Literature (1:1-3)

These opening verses establish three key aspects of Revelation that shape how we read it.

### 1. What Kind or Genre of Literature Are We Reading?

Verse 1 introduces the document as "the revelation of Jesus Christ." The word *revelation* could be translated as "apocalypse," "unveiling," or "disclosing." It is made up of a couple of Greek words that literally mean to "take out of hiding." While apocalyptic or revelatory literature can seem strange to us, it was well known in the ancient world. In the Hebrew Bible, it occurs, for example, in Daniel 7–12; Isaiah 24–27; and Zechariah 9–14. Other apocalyptic writings not in the Hebrew Bible include *1 Enoch*, *2 Baruch*, and *4 Ezra*. The last two were written after 70 C.E., about the same time as Revelation. This sort of literature often emerges from a context of crisis, or, more specifically, from a situation that the author perceives to be a crisis. It claims to "take out of hiding," reveal, or make known or disclose God's purposes for this situation.

Identifying the work's genre as apocalyptic literature creates

16

expectations. Readers would expect apocalyptic or revelatory literature to describe visions or journeys into the heavenlies.

- They would expect it to describe and expose a dualistic conflict at work among human beings between cosmic forces, between God and the devil.

- They would expect it to "take out of hiding," or disclose, the evil nature of the present world marked by oppressive political and economic structures, the power of evil forces, and sinful social interactions.

- They would expect it to reveal God's purposes and plans for the world.

- They would expect it to show that God's rule will prevail over evil and over wicked rulers no matter how powerful and destructive they seem to be.

- They would expect it to reveal the punishment of the wicked, and the blessed destiny of the righteous.

- They would expect it to describe the ultimate establishment of justice, often in a world re-created in right relationship with God. This "end," or goal, frequently resembles the beginning of the world in the same way the garden of Eden does.

- They would expect imaginative writing with strange creatures, numbers, vivid colors, conflict, and heavenly scenes.

Central to apocalyptic writing is a concern with the question of sovereignty: who or what rules the world? What is God doing, if anything, in the world that seems, at least to the writer, to have run amok? Does evil have the final word? Is there any justice for the powerless and oppressed? *Can* and *will* God intervene on their behalf? Is God faithful to God's life-giving promises? What is the goal or purpose of human existence? The use of the term *revelation*, or *apocalypse*, at the start of the writing directs our attention to these sorts of questions and signals that the writing will engage these sorts of concerns.

Revelation, then, is an apocalyptic or revelatory writing. As we read it, we need to focus on the key question, what does Revelation reveal?

17

Verse 3 creates a further set of expectations by naming another genre. Revelation is also a prophecy. We noted in the last chapter that the term *prophecy* in the biblical tradition does not primarily refer to predicting the future as it is commonly used in popular speech. Rather, it refers to speaking God's word to a particular situation. Prophets like Amos or Jeremiah place contemporary situations and behaviors in God's perspective. They interpret history and analyze current events in the context of God's purposes. They discern and address a word of God to these situations. That word might expose and rebuke sin, whether by individuals, institutions, or the powerful and wealthy. It might announce God's punishment on either the leaders or people, or both, or on other nations. It might outline a vision for the future or declare the final destiny of God's creation. The description of Revelation as "the prophecy" directs attention to these matters and creates expectations that Revelation will engage these sorts of issues.

## 2. The Source of the Revelation and Prophecy

Verse 1 declares God to be the source or origin of the revelation. God gave it to Jesus to show to others, especially John. The phrase "the revelation of Jesus Christ" can mean several things: that the revelation is about Jesus, that it belongs to Jesus, and that it comes from Jesus. All are true since this opening chapter presents Jesus as God's agent in revealing and carrying out God's purposes. God reveals the revelation to Jesus, who reveals it to an angel, who reveals it to John, who writes it down for the seven churches (and us) to read. These opening verses present the writing as authoritative, as divinely sanctioned, as a revelation of God's purposes and will. Such an authoritative framing of the book indicates that it presents a perspective about separation from the world with which some in the churches do not agree.

## 3. The Author

Verse 1 identifies John as the author of Revelation. His chief credential for being author is not that he did well in writing classes in school but that God has chosen him. God sent an angel to pass on the revelation to him. John is described as God's "servant," one who is faithfully obedient to God. This term links him with other prominent figures in the biblical tradition who are identified as God's "servants" such as Abraham (Gen 26:24), Moses (Exod 14:31), David (2 Sam 7:5, 8, 20-21, 25-26), the prophets (Amos 3:7), Daniel (Dan 6:20), and of course Jesus (Matt 12:18). This presentation aligns John closely with God and gives his message authority. John testifies to God's "word," or purposes, manifest in "the testimony of Jesus Christ" (1:2).

Just who this John is is not clear. While some in the second century understood him to be John the apostle and son of Zebedee, he does not identify himself in these ways. It is not clear how well known he is to the seven churches.

One thing we can conclude about John, though, is that he thinks the world is out of sorts. His use of apocalyptic and prophetic genres indicates that he perceives there to be a crisis in the seven churches and in the world. As we will see in discussing Revelation 2 and 3, some or many in the churches do not agree. They feel no such sense of crisis. Revelation sets about the difficult task of revealing the crisis nature of the present world to believers, many of whom seem to be quite happy with the world.

Verse 3 identifies another person involved in passing on the revelation. It blesses "the one who reads aloud the words of the prophecy." Many people in the ancient world could not read, and nobody carried a personal copy of the Bible. This unnamed figure, called a lector or reader, would read texts to the assembled believers. He or she, therefore, would have considerable influence in a congregation. Placing God's blessing on the readers of Revelation encourages them to read this revelation and pass along its message. And further authority is given to the writing by announcing God's blessing on those who "hear and keep what is written." This blessing, or beatitude, underlines the work's claim to reveal God's desire for the believers not to be involved in their Rome-ruled world.

## A Letter from God to the Seven Churches (1:4-8)

Revelation's third genre, the letter, appears in verses 4-8. Verse 4a employs the standard features of a letter, features that we know from Paul's letters. It begins by identifying the writer ("John") and then the recipients ("seven churches that are in Asia"). Chapters 2 and 3 identify these seven churches by name, as does 1:11. Some have suggested that the number seven is also to be understood symbolically. Since there were at least three other churches in the same area (Troas, 2 Cor 2:12; Colossae, Col 1:2; Hierapolis, Col 4:13), the number seven may depict "wholeness," indicating that this is a revelation for all churches. Verses 4b-8 elaborate the standard greeting ("grace and peace") by naming God (1:4, 8) and Jesus (1:5-7) as their source.

In verse 4 God is described in terms of time and power. God is the one "who is and who was and who is to come" (Rev 1:4). These phrases cover all time. They suggest that the divine purposes for the world revealed in Revelation embrace all time from the beginning to their imminent end. Associated with God are "the seven spirits who are before his throne." The reference to God's "throne" highlights God's power and rule. The mention of the "seven spirits" suggests God's ruling, powerful activity that extends to the whole world. This initial presentation of God reveals that the whole world and all of human history are in God's control despite the everyday appearance of Roman control in the seven cities.

This theme of "he's got the whole world in his hands" continues in the second reference to God in verse 8. " 'I am the Alpha and the Omega,' says the Lord God, who is and who was and who is to come, the Almighty." The phrase "I am" is the language of God's self-disclosure. God discloses Godself to Moses in the burning bush with the words, "I AM WHO I AM" (Exod 3:14). This self-disclosure sets in motion the liberation of the people from Egyptian rule. Isaiah uses the same self-disclosing language for God in rescuing the people from exile in Babylon (see Isa 41:10; 43:3, 15, 25). "Alpha and Omega" are the first and last letters of the Greek alphabet ("from A to Z"). They signify, as with the language in verse 4, the beginning and the end of all time. The verse asserts that God is active in human affairs, in control of all things, the past, present, and future, the beginning and the end. The phrase "who is and who was and who is to come" (1:4) expresses the same totality of the reach of God's purposes. In addition to embracing all time, God also has all power. God is "the Almighty," the sovereign Lord of all things.

This presentation of God reveals God's control over all things and that the whole world, including human destiny, is, despite all appearances to the contrary, in God's hands, not Rome's.

Sandwiched in between these affirmations about God in verses 4 and 8 are a series of declarations about Jesus (1:5-7). He is presented as the faithful agent and revealer of God the Almighty. Predictably the affirmations emphasize Jesus' power. He is

- "the faithful witness" (1:5). Jesus' faithful witness to God's presence includes his death on a Roman cross (1:6; 5:5). The Greek word for "witness" is *martys,* which comes to mean one who gives one's life in faithful service to God ("martyr").

- "the firstborn of the dead" (1:5): Jesus is the risen one. His resurrection from the dead signals that Roman power, the dominant power in the world, was not powerful enough to keep Jesus dead or thwart God's life-giving purposes. Jesus' resurrection anticipates the general resurrection of those who share his faithfulness. The notion of resurrection emerged in a time of oppression as an understanding that God's faithfulness was encountered beyond death in a new age in which the faithful experienced God's life-giving power and justice (compare 2 Macc 6–7).

- "ruler of the kings of the earth" (1:5): Jesus is the supreme, universal, powerful ruler exercising God's rule (1:4). He, not the emperor, despite imperial claims, controls the world.

- the one who lovingly delivers from sin (1:5): This fourth affirmation comes in the form of a doxology, or declaration of praise. Jesus is praised for freeing people from sin through his death ("blood"), and for loving us. The rest of Revelation will reveal that sin is not understood only as individual or personal sins but also as the sins of the Roman imperial system (ch. 18, for example).

- the one who creates a people to serve God (1:6): This people seems to comprise followers of Jesus. They are identified first as a "kingdom" or "empire." These people share Jesus' ruling power and comprise an alternative community with alternative allegiances and loyalties in the midst of Rome's empire. Their alternative allegiances are expressed in being a community of priests who serve God and who mediate God's blessings to

21

others. As Revelation progresses, there is some suggestion that all people are drawn into the community that serves God (5:13; 15:4; 21:24-26).

- the one who has "glory and dominion for ever and ever" (1:6): The doxology recognizes that Jesus shares in God's power and rule forever.

- the one who will return to earth to rule over all: Verse 7 presents Jesus as the one who will return to establish God's rule at the end of time, known as "the eschaton." It combines a reference to the Son of Man in Daniel 7, who represents God's rule, with a passage from Zech 12:10 interpreted in terms of Jesus' crucifixion. God's purposes will prevail over all things.

Verses 5-7 declare Jesus' power in terms of his overcoming death and sin, of out-powering all earthly rulers, of creating a special people, and of controlling the destiny of the world. He, along with God, is the source of the grace and peace that John mediates to his readers in Revelation. He holds the whole world, its origin and destiny, in his hands.

## John as the Authorized Revealer of God (1:9-20)

Accounts of the words and ministry of a prophet often include a call, or commission, story. A call story gives an account of how God called this person to a special role as a prophet. The burning bush story is one such example, in which God spoke to the shepherd Moses and commissioned him to lead the people out of Egyptian slavery (Exod 3). Isaiah provided an account of his vision of God in the Temple in which God commissioned him to speak to the people (Isa 6). Jeremiah claimed to be called as a prophet to the nations while in his mother's womb (Jer 1:4-10). Ezekiel described an elaborate call vision (Ezek 1–3). These narratives legitimate the prophet as one authorized by God.

This section in Rev 1:9-20 sanctions John as God's revealer. It describes the vision and audition in which the risen Jesus calls John to his role as God's prophet and spokesperson. We can note four dimensions of John's call to be a prophet.

*1:9—John's context:* John begins by stressing his solidarity "in Jesus" with his readers as his brothers and sisters. They share "affliction." The word is often translated "persecution," but this is not accurate. In Revelation the word has a more general meaning. In 2:9-10 it is linked with poverty, in 2:22 and 7:14 with hardship. John shares membership with his readers in God's kingdom or empire (so 1:6). They share "patient endurance," a quality that occurs seven times in Revelation. "Patient endurance" embraces work (2:2), bearing up and not growing weary (2:3), "love, faith, service" (2:19), loyalty (3:10), and keeping God's commandments and being faithful to Jesus (14:12). That is, John finds solidarity with the other Jesus-believers in being faithful to God.

John says his vision occurred when he was on the small island of Patmos off the coast of southwest Asia Minor. Contrary to what is often claimed, he does not say he was exiled or banished there. He was not being persecuted for preaching. There is no evidence for such persecution or for Patmos being a place of punishment. John says he is on Patmos "because of the word of God and the testimony of Jesus." Was he preaching there? Or was he on retreat for renewal? We do not know.

*1:10-11—the command:* During worship he hears a "loud voice" (1:10). The "loud voice" instructs him to "write...what you see and send it to the seven churches." The seven churches are probably listed in the order that a messenger would visit them with this writing. From Ephesus, the messenger would go north to Smyrna and Pergamum before turning south to visit the rest.

*1:12-18—the risen Christ as the caller:* The identity of the one with the loud voice is not disclosed until verses 17-18. John prepares for that identification by presenting the figure in terms that suggest divine presence and power. He is, for example, "one like the Son of Man" (Rev 1:13). This term echoes Dan 7:13, which the author evoked previously in verse 7. In the vision of Daniel 7, a heavenly, or angelic, being in human form appears as the representative of God's "everlasting dominion" (7:27) and "kingship...that shall never be destroyed" (Dan 7:14). The figure that John sees wears garments that recall descriptions of both heavenly beings, or angels, and priests. His white head and hair recall the description

23

of God in Dan 7:9. Fire, associated with his eyes, also suggests divine presence, as does the description of the voice as being "like the sound of mighty waters" (Ezek 1:24).

This passage is typical of Revelation's style. Like a music video, it heaps up image after image. It builds a collage-like impression of divine majesty and power. It assumes that we know what these images signify, particularly though not exclusively from our knowledge of the Hebrew Bible. Revelation does not stop and explain each image to us.

John describes being overawed by this figure and falls at his feet in submission. The symbolic nature of the scene is seen in that the figure holds stars in his right hand while also using his right hand to touch John. The right is the side of favor and blessing, the left the side of misfortune and curse (which does not sound good for us left-handers!). The figure speaks, first assuring John not to be afraid (as heavenly figures commonly do in the Bible—see Gen 15:1-2; 21:17; 26:24; Josh 11:6; Matt 1:20; Luke 1:13, 30). Then using the "I am" language of divine self-disclosure (see 1:8), the figure discloses his identity. As "the first and the last" (1:17) he spans all history and time, the beginning and end of human history (again compare 1:8). As the one who was dead but is now "alive forever and ever," he is clearly the risen exalted Christ who, having been crucified, now rules over the power of death wielded by the Roman Empire (Hades is the place of the dead).

*1:19-20—John's commission:* This commission repeats the command of 1:11 to "write what you have seen, what is, and what is to take place after this."

The exalted Christ then offers an explanation for two aspects of the vision. He explains that "the seven stars that you saw in my right hand" refer to "the angels of the seven churches." The word translated "angels" can mean "messenger" and can refer to human beings (so Luke 9:52), so it could be that these "messengers of the seven churches" are the leaders of each of the seven churches. However, it seems more likely that heavenly beings are in mind. The term *angel* elsewhere in Revelation usually refers to heavenly beings. And apocalyptic literature often presents earthly realities as having heavenly counterparts. So in Daniel, for example, each nation has a heavenly angel as its counterpart. As the nations fight each other, so do their "guardian" (heavenly) angels. Michael fights against the prince of Persia and then Greece (Dan 10:12-21; also 11:1; 12:1). These factors suggest that the "seven stars" as the "angels of the seven churches" refer to heavenly beings, are the counterparts of the earthly churches. What is most significant, though, is that the exalted Christ has them in his hand. These heavenly beings are in his control and all-embracing power.

The second explanation concerns the seven lampstands. These were first mentioned in 1:13, when the one like the Son of Man first appeared in their midst. Now the exalted Christ declares them to be "the seven churches" to which the revelation is addressed. The significant point is that not only does he have their heavenly counterparts in his right hand but the exalted Christ is also in the midst of and present with the churches whom John addresses.

# Conclusion

The opening chapter of Revelation has established John as the authorized, sanctioned recipient of a revelation from God and the exalted Christ, to be addressed to the churches in the seven cities in the Roman province of Asia. It has presented John's call to be God's revealer and prophet. The risen and exalted Jesus appeared to John and told him to write to the seven churches. This "call narrative" lends great authority to what John writes. The message is that the hearers in the churches had better listen up. Moreover, in describing God and Jesus, the chapter repeatedly asserts their power and control in the midst of the Roman Empire. The chapter reveals that they have the whole world and the seven churches in their hands.

# Study Questions

1. If someone asked you what was interesting about Revelation 1, what would you say?

2. If the writer of Revelation were to be hired as an "Apocalyptic Visionary," how would chapter 1 show him doing his job?

25

3. If the writer of Revelation were to be hired as a prophet, how would chapter 1 show him doing his job?

4. How does the chapter establish John's authority as God's spokesperson?

CHAPTER 3

# Revelation Reveals That Cultural Accommodation Is Dangerous, Part 1 (Rev 2:1-17)

In Revelation 2–3 we move from the island of Patmos, where John experiences his vision, to the churches in seven cities in the Roman province of Asia. We move from John's vision of the exalted Christ to the daily realities of seven churches that the exalted Christ addresses. At the heart of these letters is conflict between John and other Jesus groups that John calls "Balaamites," "Nicolaitans," and followers of "Jezebel." The issue in contention concerns how Jesus-believers should participate in their urban societies. The letters reveal that their cultural accommodation, with which many are quite comfortable, is dangerous.

Chapters 2–3 comprise seven letters. Each letter is both specific and general in its address. That is, the letters are addressed to specific churches and address matters specific to that church. Yet they are included in the general letter that is Revelation (1:4). Therefore they are part of what the Spirit is saying to "the churches" (plural; 2:7, 11, 17), and are available to every reader of Revelation.

The letters largely follow the same format (see next page).

From the chart we can notice that all of them begin with an address to the angel that is the heavenly counterpart of each church. John is instructed to write "the words of" the risen Christ (1:3). The risen Christ is described in various ways that often recall John's vision from chapter 1. Particularly the focus on "the words"

27

| | Ephesus | Smyrna | Pergamum | Thyatira | Sardis | Philadelphia | Laodicea |
|---|---|---|---|---|---|---|---|
| To the angel | 2:1a | 2:8a | 2:12a | 2:18a | 3:1a | 3:7a | 3:14a |
| Church | 2:1b | 2:8b | 2:12b | 2:18b | 3:1b | 3:7b | 3:14b |
| Write | 2:1c | 2:8c | 2:12c | 2:18c | 3:1c | 3:7c | 3:14c |
| The words | 2:1d | 2:8d | 2:12d | 2:18d | 3:1d | 3:7d | 3:14d |
| Descriptor | 2:1e | 2:8e | 2:12e | 2:18e | 3:1e | 3:7e | 3:14e |
| I know | 2:2a | 2:9a | 2:13a | 2:19a | 3:1f | 3:8a | 3:15a |
| Commend | 2:2b-3, 6 | 2:9b | 2:13b | 2:19, 24 | 3:4 | 3:8b-10 | |
| Rebuke | 2:4-5a | | 2:14-15 | 2:20-23 | 3:1g-2 | | 3:15b-20 |
| Exhort | | 2:10 | | 2:25 | 3:3a-b | 3:11 | |
| Repent | 2:5b | | 2:16a | 2:21-22(?) | 3:3c | | 3:19c |
| Threatened judgment | 2:5b | | 2:16b | 2:23 | 3:3d | | 3:16b |
| Listen | 2:7a | 2:11a | 2:17a | 2:29 | 3:6 | 3:13 | 3:20a,22 |
| Conquers | 2:7b | 2:11b | 2:17b | 2:26-28 | 3:5a | 3:12a | 3:21a |
| Promise of life | 2:7c | 2:10c, 11c | 2:17c | 2:28 | 3:4, 5b | 3:12b | 3:21b |

recalls the description of the exalted Christ in 1:16 from whose "mouth came a sharp, two-edged sword." These "words" are the means by which Revelation does its revealing work. It also recalls the authoritative formula "Thus says the LORD," found in prophetic writings (Jer 2:1-4). In this tradition, as in the creation story ("Then God said," Gen 1:3), God's word is powerfully effective in accomplishing God's purposes.

Then, as the chart shows, in each letter, the good, the bad, or the ugly follow as the seven churches are variously praised, commended, blamed, rebuked, and exhorted. The central issue concerns how believers should live in their urban contexts. Five of the churches are commanded to repent and threatened with judgment. Each letter closes with exhortations to listen to what the Spirit is saying to the churches, and with promises of life or participation in God's final, or eschatological, purposes.

We will look at each letter in turn. In this chapter we will discuss the first three letters to the churches in Ephesus, Smyrna, and Pergamum, leaving the other four letters to the next chapter.

## Ephesus (2:1-7)

Ephesus was the capital city of the Roman province of Asia, an important center of political, administrative, cultural, and economic power. Because of its port, it was an important trading and commercial center. The city's patron goddess was the ever-present Artemis, whose temple (one of the Seven Wonders of the World) was a significant economic, cultural, and political force in the city, in alliance with Roman imperial power. An imperial temple was dedicated in Ephesus in 88/89 C.E. around the time Revelation was written.

The risen Christ presents himself to the Ephesians as the one "who holds the seven stars in his right hand, who walks among the seven golden lampstands" (2:1). This description builds on John's commissioning vision in 1:9-20 in which the risen Christ holds these seven stars (1:16) and is in the midst of the lampstands (1:13). That vision explained that the seven stars are the heavenly angelic counterparts of the churches and the lampstands are the churches themselves (1:20). The repetition of these identities at the

29

outset of the letter underlines the power and presence of the exalted Christ in addressing the church at Ephesus through John's words.

This power and presence is the basis for his "knowing" about the church (2:2a). Verses 2-3 praise the church for its faithful discipleship, "your works, your toil and your patient endurance." But a specific issue also emerges.

It has resisted "evildoers" who "claim to be apostles but are not, and have found them to be false" (2:2). The reference to "apostles" suggests there has been a leadership struggle involving these figures. They seem to have been teaching different things. There have been divisions among church members in response to these figures. Unfortunately, the letter is not clear about the details and consequences. Are there still divisions? Are some still committed to this teaching? What has happened to these "false" teachers, now that they have been excluded from the Ephesian church? If they were itinerant teachers, they may well have moved on to another congregation. Did some of the Ephesian believers follow them? Whatever the details, John commends the Ephesians (or at least some of them) for discerning that these figures were, in the writer's opinion, "false apostles."

Clearly the author does not envision a church in which multiple beliefs and practices can coexist. There is no room for diversity of thinking and practice. The commendation ends with more general praise for "enduring patiently and bearing up for the sake of my name, and that you have not grown weary" (2:3).

But despite this commendation, all is not well. The commendation is followed in verses 4-5a with a rebuke. He says that while the Ephesian church had begun well, it has "abandoned the love you had at first." Whether this love refers to members' devotion for God, or one another, or neighbors, or all of these is not specified. What does seem to be at issue is that of priority, of vital and active discipleship, of a distinctive and loyal way of life. For whatever reasons—perhaps "the cares and riches and pleasures of life" (Luke 8:14)—their vibrancy of lived faithfulness has been lost. How Jesus-believers relate to and participate in their urban society so as not to compromise their commitment to Christ will emerge as the key issue through the chapter. They are instructed to "repent," which means changing their lifestyle so that they "do the works you did at first." Love shapes a distinctive Christian way of life. Without it there is no church. That will be their judgment.

Verse 6 returns to commendation while revealing a struggle: "you hate the works of the Nicolaitans, which I also hate." Are the false apostles mentioned in verse 2 the Nicolaitans? Or is this a separate group? Interestingly, the present tense used for "you hate" suggests an ongoing conflict, and that not everyone in the Ephesian church has "hated" the Nicolaitans. The Nicolaitans are mentioned again in the letter to Pergamum in 2:14-15, where we learn more about them. We will discuss them further there. It is sufficient here to note that part of the struggle with the Nicolaitans concerns the question of faithful discipleship and how involved followers of Jesus should be in the practices and institutions of their city and society, where idols and images were a common part of everyday life. Perhaps in this light, the author thinks the loss of the love they had at first (2:4) means some have become too comfortable, too much at home, too accommodated in their city's way of life. He disapproves of such social conformity and wants much more distinctiveness and distance.

The letter concludes with an exhortation to understand and a promise to those who "conquer" (2:7). The verb *conquer* recurs regularly in Revelation. It denotes those who remain faithful to the exalted Christ in distinctive and active discipleship. Their reward is to participate in the end-time, full establishment of God's purposes, known as the eschaton. Eschatological visions—visions of the full and final establishment of God's purposes—take numerous forms at the close of each letter. Here the reference to "[eating] from the tree of life...in the paradise of God," echoes the garden of Eden story (see Gen 2:17; 3:1-19) and envisions the reversal of the impact of sin and death. That is, it promises participation in the restoration of a world like that of the garden of Eden, without sin and in which all is ordered according to God's life-giving purposes.

## Smyrna (2:8-11)

With this short letter, we move north from Ephesus about thirty-five miles to another harbor city. This letter, like that to

Philadelphia, has no rebuke or threat of judgment. Nevertheless the letter indicates that the church is involved in significant conflict.

The risen Christ presents himself in echoes of 1:17-18 as the one who embraces all time and all things, and who has overcome death inflicted by Roman power ("the first and the last, who was dead and came to life," 2:8). As with the address to the Ephesians, this description underlines the power and authority of the exalted Christ to whom the Smyrnan believers have entrusted themselves.

The risen Christ recognizes "your affliction and your poverty, even though you are rich" (2:9). Their poverty is material; they lack everyday necessities including, at times, food. Most people in the ancient world were poor. By contrast they are rich in faith and good works.

They also experience "affliction." This "affliction" is elaborated in the next sentence as "the slander on the part of those who say that they are Jews and are not, but are a synagogue of Satan." This is harsh polemical language born out of a conflictual situation. We should remember that given the extensive use of Hebrew Bible images in Revelation (e.g., 5:5 for Jesus), it seems likely that a significant number of the Jesus-believers were Jews. It is very likely that Jesus-believers in Smyrna composed a group within the synagogue.

The details of the conflict are not clear. Does the slander center on a refusal by some in the synagogue to confess Jesus' identity? Does it concern slander over the definition of the term "Jew"? Are Jesus-believers claiming to be the true Jews and the exclusive heirs to Israel's promises, which non-Jesus-believing Jews rightly found very offensive?

There is another possibility suggested by the struggle with the Nicolaitans in Ephesus and to which we will return in the next letter. Perhaps John considers the behavior of some or many in the synagogue community to be slanderous because he thought it faithless. We know from various data that Jews were active participants in their first-century urban contexts and civic structures. They participated in trade and commerce, gathered in the theater, held political office, spoke Greek, engaged in Greek education in the gymnasium, participated in actions that honored a range of elite figures from local city administrators to the emperor, belonged to trade associations, promoted their own community's well-being with gifts, and attracted Gentile sympathizers to synagogue communities. Perhaps some also participated in the celebration of Roman power based in the temple dedicated to the emperor Tiberius. Prayers and sacrifices to various gods and goddesses, and images of divinities and of Roman imperial figures pervaded every aspect of civic life. Participation in such observances was not mandatory but avoiding them was difficult. Jews of course also observed distinctive Jewish practices such as Sabbath observance, contributions to the Jerusalem Temple, and study of the tradition (Torah). But they were not isolated enclaves of "pure" and withdrawn Jewish identity. Their boundaries with the urban environments were quite fluid and porous.

Perhaps John thinks that some or many in the synagogue, along with Jesus-believers who imitated their lifestyle as part of synagogue communities, had become too culturally accommodated. Perhaps he thought that they were too familiar with honoring idols and images, that they were faithless to their identity of being God's distinctive people. Hence he declares that they are not really Jews because he considers them to be faithless to their heritage (2:9). He calls them a "synagogue of Satan" because he considers them to be faithless to God. This hateful language—which we must remember is John's perspective and not "fact"—reflects his attempt to clarify a situation he considers too ambiguous, porous, and compromised. Assuming that this synagogue included Jesus-believers, it suggests that some Jesus-believers lived in similar accommodated ways and are included in John's condemnation.

John, though, seems to recognize that, in Smyrna at least, more of the believers distanced themselves from these practices. While there seem to have been differences or conflict among the Jesus-believers over how (much) to participate in their cultural context, John is generally positive about the church in Smyrna.

We should note that this abusive language about the synagogue as belonging to Satan emerges from a particular conflictual situation. Its presence in this biblical material certainly offers no sanction for contemporary Christians to speak about Jews—or anyone else—in these terms. Its presence in our sacred writings is a cause for lament and sadness by contemporary Christians.

Whatever the dispute is about, John warns Smyrnans in 2:10

about future trouble. "Do not fear what you are about to suffer. Beware, the devil is about to throw some of you into prison so that you may be tested, and for ten days you will have affliction. Be faithful until death." Just what circumstances are in view for this limited time of suffering ("for ten days") is not at all clear. There was no legal penalty for being a Christian. Perhaps the refusal by some believers to participate in civic rituals caused problems. One possibility is that refusing to participate was seen as risking the displeasure of the gods or the Romans, or both, thereby endangering the city with the risk of reprisals. It is helpful to remember that we are reading religious polemic here, the perspective of one person fighting against another group and perspective, where intense emotion rather than factual accuracy dominates.

The letter ends in 2:11 with a double promise of life or eschatological reward for those who remain faithful even "until death." Faithfulness "conquers" means that they will escape the "second death," an image that Revelation later uses to indicate the final (eschatological) destruction of the wicked (20:6, 14), who do not participate in the full and final establishment of God's purposes. The "crown of life" (2:10) signifies participation in these purposes.

## Pergamum (2:12-17)

Fifty miles north of Sardis is Pergamum. This city was the site for a famous library and a large altar dedicated to Zeus on which animal sacrifices were offered. This altar was more than one hundred feet wide and can be seen today in a museum in Berlin. There were numerous other temples there, including those dedicated to the god of healing, Asclepius, which attracted sick folks hoping for a healing appearance of the god. The complex issue of how Jesus-believers negotiated daily life in the Roman province of Asia is also to the fore in this letter.

The risen Christ is again described in terms borrowed from 1:16 that emphasize the power of his words (1:12). He recognizes the challenges of living "where Satan's throne is" (2:13). Whether this refers to the altar of Zeus or imperial celebrations or multiple dimensions of urban life is not clear. As with the letter to Smyrna, John quickly draws an "either-or" world and immediately links

34

those whom he opposes with the devil. The dualism that the letter tries to create is clearly not the same as the complex reality that the church experiences in everyday life.

After the introduction, John commends them for their loyal and steadfast faith, even in the previous time when Antipas was killed. No information about Antipas is provided, though John again links those responsible for it with Satan ("where Satan lives," 2:14). We should note that Antipas is the only actual martyr that Revelation identifies (apart from Jesus).

Verse 14 expresses the rebuke. It is directed not against the whole church but against "some there." Some "hold to the teaching of Balaam, who taught Balak to put a stumbling block before the people of Israel, so that they would eat food sacrificed to idols and practice fornication." And some "hold to the teaching of the Nicolaitans" (2:15), who were mentioned as being active in Ephesus (2:6). The initial wording of verse 15 ("so") indicates that the Nicolaitans are to be identified with "the teaching of Balaam."

This rebuke makes explicit what seemed to be a likely dimension of the conflict with the synagogue in Smyrna and the loss of first love in Ephesus. The "teaching of Balaam" probably refers not to Balaam blessing Israel (Num 22–24), but to other traditions about Balaam found in Jewish writings other than the biblical writings (Philo, *Life of Moses* 1.292-304; Josephus, *Antiquities* 4.126-158). These traditions linked Balaam to the subsequent episode in Numbers 25 involving idolatry with the god Baal of Peor and Israelite men marrying Midianite women. In the resulting war, Balaam is killed as God's punishment for being responsible for Israel's idolatry ("the affair of Peor," Num 31:16). On the basis of this reference to Balaam's activity, some in the church at Pergamum, it seems, were teaching that it is OK for Jesus-believers to be involved in numerous civic activities that included honoring idols and images (prayers, sacrifices, festivals, games, meals).

John's complaint is with two particular activities, eating food offered to idols and "fornication." Eating food offered to idols refers to the various contexts in which eating food dedicated to idols took place: food that had been consecrated to particular deities and sold in the market or by street vendors (cf. 1 Cor 8–10), meat sacrificed and then eaten in the presence of an idol in a temple, or a meal eaten by a trade or guild association (to which many artisans, merchants, and laborers belonged) that included offerings to deities and images. The link between food and its dedication to idols was extensive. Belonging to trade associations was a crucial networking strategy for many artisans, craftsmen, merchants, and laborers. How were Jesus-believers to feed themselves in the city? How were they to secure work? John disapproves of the involvements with idols that pervaded daily life.

The term "fornication" is probably to be understood metaphorically rather than as literal sexual behavior. Prophets use the metaphor to condemn idolatrous behavior that they saw as forsaking covenant commitments and participating in the ways of Gentile cultures, including idolatry (Ezek 16:15, 34; Hos 4:10-19). So in Ps 106:35, Israel "mingled with the nations and learned to do as they did. They served their idols," actions that in Ps 106:39 constitute their "committing fornication in their doings" (author's translation).

Revelation's three other uses of the verb to "commit fornication" condemn participation in Gentile culture, notably Rome's empire. Three uses appear in chapters 17–18 to celebrate the condemnation of Babylon, a code name for Rome. Rome's client-kings, or rulers of subordinated peoples, have participated culturally, politically, economically, and religiously in imperial culture (17:2; 18:3, 9). They have allied themselves with Rome's political power, upholding and benefiting from the hierarchical status quo whereby the small ruling elite, both Roman and provincial, sustained their existence at the expense of the vast majority of the nonelite poor. Client-kings participated in Rome's economy through trade, taxes, tributes, and patronage. They participated in various festivals that were an integral part of imperial life, offering prayers and sacrifices to imperial images; sponsoring feasts, festivals, and games; and performing the roles of priests and priestesses. This "idolatry" pervaded every part of daily life.

John's complaint is that some in the church are participating too much in their urban civic context and compromise their commitment to Christ. Perhaps some have eaten food in temples or in the regular gathering of guild associations where sacrifices to idols have been offered. Perhaps some have participated in the numerous festivals for deities and imperial figures that pervaded civic life. Festivals honoring deities and Roman imperial figures took place in temples—like the altar of Zeus, the imperial temple in Pergamum, or the temple of Artemis in Ephesus—as well as in other public civic spaces such as squares, theaters, the stadia or gymnasia, and baths where images and altars could be located. Festivals involved offering prayers and hymns, sacrifices, processions, games, and feasts. Such observances of deities and imperial power pervaded these cities in Asia. Religion was not regarded as a "private" and "personal" activity separated from every other aspect of life. Participation in these activities was not required but everybody joined in. Such festivals and observances were not isolated religious activities separated from other societal spheres. Rather, observances were enmeshed in daily political, economic, and social interactions. To separate oneself from such civic activities and association gatherings meant losing social and economic connections and benefits.

How are Jesus-believers to live in a context where religious and political observances are enmeshed in every aspect of daily life? There is a dispute among the Jesus-believers about the issue. Some (the Balaamites and Nicolaitans) argue that active and involved participation is fine and harmless. John does not agree. He reveals that such activity is idolatry. It is as false as "fornication." It is from such activities that John wants the Jesus-believers to separate and distance themselves, no matter the cost. Revelation reveals the danger of cultural accommodation.

John's vision of a faithful church does not allow for diverse practices and thinking about societal participation. Accordingly, he demands that those listening to the Balaamites and Nicolaitans change their ways and repent. He supports this demand by warning that the risen Christ will condemn those who do not separate. He appeals to the authority of the Spirit (3:16-17a), and to the promise that only those who "conquer" (or faithfully live out John's demands) will participate in the fullness of God's purposes. An image of eating again denotes those purposes (so 2:7). This time the manna that God provided for the people escaping from the Egyptians in the exodus will be on the menu for the final banquet. A "white stone" may well be the admission ticket to this feast. A "new name" signifies a new identity in God's purposes (2:17).

# Conclusion

The letters of chapter 2 present cultural participation as the dominant issue facing these churches. The churches are not unified in their practice or thinking about this issue. The letters attack those Jesus-believers who think it is legitimate and harmless to participate in their urban society, where both the influence of and the honoring of idols and images are pervasive. The letters make multiple appeals to divine authority to sanction John's call to societal separation and distance. They reveal that cultural accommodation is dangerous.

# Study Questions

1. What, according to John, is going on in the churches in Ephesus, Smyrna, and Pergamum? Do their strengths and weaknesses resemble your own church's life in any way?

2. What are some of the idolatries and places of unfaithfulness in our contemporary efforts to live as faithful disciples?

3. What are some present-day examples of cultural accommodation? Are they dangerous? Necessary? Both? How do you navigate through the complexity of these issues?

# CHAPTER 4

# Revelation Reveals That Cultural Accommodation Is Dangerous, Part 2 (Rev 2:18–3:22)

In the last chapter we looked at the letters addressed in Revelation 2 to the churches in Ephesus, Smyrna, and Pergamum. Four more letters to churches in the Roman province of Asia (modern-day Turkey) follow in the rest of Revelation 2–3. The same complex issue of participating in their daily cultural worlds continues to be prominent. Revelation continues to reveal that cultural accommodation is dangerous.

## Thyatira (2:18-29)

From Pergamum the carrier of Revelation headed southeast to the trading city of Thyatira. Its numerous guilds (wool-workers, linen weavers, leather workers, dyers, tailors, shoemakers, bakers, etc.) attest the city's typical commercial activity. The risen Christ is introduced as God's agent ("Son of God," 2:18) with fiery eyes (cf. 1:14) and bronzed feet, depicting vigilance, presence, and power. The church is commended for "love, faith, service, and patient endurance."

The rebuke for the church at Thyatira is very similar to that of the church at Pergamum in 2:12-17. It concerns the same question of how to participate in a society that has very different commitments. The rebuke centers on "that woman Jezebel, who calls herself a prophet and is teaching and beguiling my servants to practice fornication and to eat food sacrificed to idols" (2:20). "Jezebel" is a significant church leader who advocates the same cultural participation as the Balaamites and Nicolaitans, so strongly condemned in 2:6 (Ephesus) and 2:14-15 (Pergamum). Predictably, John is not tolerant of her teaching and of diverse thinking and practices in the churches.

The name "Jezebel" is not the real name of this church leader. This nickname is one aspect of John's sustained attempt to present her negatively as an opponent and to discredit her teaching that cultural and civic participation did not make the people unfaithful to God's purposes.

- The name he chooses for her, "Jezebel," evokes a woman in the Hebrew Bible who was associated with idolatry and false prophets. She was a Phoenician who married King Ahab of Israel. Jezebel and Ahab "served Baal, and worshipped him" (1 Kgs 16:31; see also 18:4, 13; 19:1-3). Ahab, "urged on by his wife Jezebel...acted most abominably in going after idols" (1 Kgs 21:25-26; see also 2 Kgs 9:22). Her bloody death is God's will (1 Kgs 21:23-24; 2 Kgs 9:30-37). As with the link to Balaam, this name, "Jezebel," presents this teacher as an opponent of John's teaching. It presents her as being divinely condemned for societal interactions and idolatrous practices contrary to the divine will.

The image of "fornication," with which "Jezebel" is associated, is related in Greek to the words *whore* or *prostitute* that Revelation uses to condemn Rome (17:1, 4). Jezebel, who approves of participation in Roman imperial culture, is condemned with Rome.

- By saying she "calls herself a prophet" (2:20), John casts doubts on her legitimacy as a teacher of God's will. True prophets do not "call themselves" prophets. God calls true prophets. John's description of her "calling herself" contrasts with the content of chapter 1, in which he sets out his own call to be a prophet.
- John calls her a "beguiler" or "deceiver" (2:20, author's translation) and thereby associates her with three very disreputable

40

figures whom Revelation later calls deceivers: the devil (12:9), the second beast (13:14), and Babylon/Rome (18:23). All are condemned by God.
• In verse 24 he calls her teaching "the deep things of Satan."

Clearly John disagrees very strongly with her teaching that active involvement in their city life pervaded by honoring idols is OK for Jesus-believers. It is easy for us to be swept along in John's rhetoric against Jezebel and to accept his condemnation of her advocacy of active participation in daily urban life as obvious and compelling. But it is worth pausing to ask, "Why did she advocate cultural participation?" That is, it's easy to get the impression that she woke up in the morning and decided quite deliberately to be as faithless as possible in misleading God's people. But this would do her a disservice.

Revelation's attack on her suggests that there was a deeply divisive debate among Jesus-believers in the churches of Asia about how they were to conduct themselves in their society. The answers were not self-evident. Why does Jezebel advocate cultural participation?

In making his own argument for separation and distance, John certainly does not devote space to presenting her viewpoint. But we might guess at some of her arguments.

1. Perhaps in a world where most people were poor and struggled for survival, she did not see cultural and socioeconomic separation as a practical option. How would people maintain separation and also support themselves and their households, since religious observances pervaded economic activity like trade and commerce?

2. Perhaps with the previous martyrdom of Antipas (2:13), she realized that refusal to participate in civic honoring and socioeconomic activities would only increase distrust and provoke hostile reprisals. It could be interpreted as disloyalty to the city gods, as tempting fate, as risking retaliation from various divinities or even imperial figures.

3. Perhaps she argued theologically and appealed to an argument Paul makes. Paul argues in 1 Corinthians that since "no idol in the world really exists" and that "there is no God but

one" (1 Cor 8:4), idols, images, and rituals with sacrifices and prayers had no power. They could not harm Jesus-believers. Therefore it was fine for Jesus-believers, knowing that Jesus is Lord, to participate in trade association meetings and activities, in civic festivals, and in gatherings in the theater where idols and images were common.

4. Perhaps she appealed to the Bible. The Bible offered examples of people who participated in imperial society, and God seemed to prosper them. For example, Joseph rose to power and prominence in Egypt (Gen 37–50). Jeremiah exhorted those taken in exile to Babylon to settle there and make it their home, to "build houses...plant gardens...take wives...[and] seek the welfare of the city...for in its welfare you will find your welfare" (Jer 29:5-7).

5. Perhaps she, like others, understood Rome's victory over Jerusalem in 70 C.E. as an indication of both the futility of rebellion and Rome's status as an empire chosen and used by God (Josephus, *Jewish War* 2.360, 390-91; 5.367-68, 378). God had used other empires like Assyria (Isa 10:5-11), Babylon (Jer 25:1-11), and Persia and its leader Cyrus (Isa 44:28; 45:1). Cultural participation in the benefits of empire would ensure the experience of God's blessing.

We do not know for sure if Jezebel made such arguments. These five possible justifications for civic involvement are only guesses. But they remind us that the issue of cultural participation was and is complex. While John's voice dominates Revelation, it is important to remember that it was not the only perspective. John wants a church with only one way of being in the world.

John's harsh rhetoric against Jezebel continues in verse 21. She has refused to "repent" or change her teaching and "fornication." That is, she does not agree with John's perspective. John declares judgment on her followers (2:22-23) and encourages the rest to "hold fast" (2:24-25). There is a sharp division in this and other churches. He promises eschatological participation to those who persevere in John's teaching ("conquers," 2:26). This participation means sharing in God's rule over all nations (2:26-27; perhaps this is the meaning of "morning star" in 2:28).

# Sardis (3:1-6)

The carrier of Revelation continued southeast some 30 miles or so to Sardis. This was also a thriving commercial center with the facilities of a major city (theater, baths, stadium, civic and business centers, temples for Artemis and Cybele, gymnasium). But while the city had life, Revelation declares the church to be dead.

The letter begins not with commendation but with rebuke. The church has the reputation of "being alive, but...dead" (3:1). They are "at the point of death, for I have not found your works perfect in the sight of my God" (3:2). Just exactly what composes this "deadness" is not made explicit, though we will get a hint in verse 4 that cultural accommodation is again the issue. In the meantime, there is a repeated exhortation to "wake up, and strengthen what remains," to "remember then what you received and heard," and to "obey it, and repent" (3:2-3). There is also a threat of judgment when the exalted Christ will come and catch them unprepared.

Verse 4 offers commendation for "a few people in Sardis who have not soiled their clothes," who "will walk with me, dressed in white, for they are worthy." The color white in Revelation denotes purity (19:14) and is usually associated with allegiance to the exalted Christ (7:9, 13-14). Accordingly, it also denotes victorious participation in the completion of God's purposes (3:5). The elders who worship in the heavenlies are clothed in white (4:4) as are those who are martyred for loyalty to God (6:11). Soiling one's clothes, then, is an image of unfaithfulness and disobedience to the exalted Christ's teaching.

We have seen in the letters in chapter 2 that Revelation urges separation from any civic activity—social, economic, religious, political—that involves any idolatrous practice. The central problem with these churches for John is that, spurred on by the teaching of teachers like "Jezebel," they are too comfortable, too accommodated, too actively participating in the socioeconomic and political practices of their religiously infused society. In John's view, they thereby compromise their loyalty to Christ and will not participate in the completion of God's purposes with the white-clad elders and martyrs. While the Balaamites, Nicolaitans, and followers of Jezebel are not mentioned, it seems the same issue impacts Sardis. In the words of the letter to the church in Ephesus, the Sardis believers have also abandoned their first love (2:4) and are dead because of their cultural accommodation. Revelation reveals that cultural accommodation is dangerous.

Repentance means "waking up," a change of lifestyle whereby they conquer, or live faithfully a distinctive and separated life (3:3). This way of life will result in their participation in the completion of God's purposes. Three images illustrate this participation. One is, as we have seen, wearing "white robes" of purity and victory (3:4). The second is having their names in "the book of life" (3:5). This image refers in the Hebrew Bible to God's registry of the faithful (Exod 32:32-33) who will experience the final victory of God (Dan 12:1). To be blotted out of this book because of continual unfaithfulness denotes judgment (Ps 69:28). The third image is that of a heavenly court in which the exalted Christ advocates for those who have separated from cultural entanglements and have lived faithfully. Christ says, "I will confess your name before my Father and before his angels" (3:5). The letter ends with the customary exhortation to listen well.

## Philadelphia (3:7-13)

Another 30 or so miles southeast of Thyatira is the smaller city of Philadelphia. There are two similarities between this letter and that to the church in Smyrna (2:8-11). Both have commendations but no rebuke. And both reference synagogue communities.

The initial description of the exalted Christ does not draw on the call vision of 1:9-20, but anticipates the content of the letter. He is presented in 3:7 as both the "holy" and "true" one, words that often describe God (6:10). Their use underlines the divine authority with which the exalted Christ speaks to the church.

He also has "the key of David," a phrase that, along with the subsequent references to "opening" and "shutting," evokes Isa 22:22. This passage from Isaiah describes a key entrusted to a steward, Eliakim, to represent his authority over the household of David, the line chosen by God to be kings and representatives of God's rule (2 Sam 7). Here the exalted Christ has authority over God's kingdom or empire, and over the church that belongs to and manifests God's rule.

The church's situation is presented positively in 3:8. The exalted Christ has "set before you an open door," an image of opportunity for bearing witness and mission according to Paul's use (1 Cor 16:9; 2 Cor 2:12). He recognizes that they have "little power," perhaps an indication of the few numbers and low social status of the believers. And they are commended for keeping "my word and have not denied my name."

Verse 9 turns attention to "those of the synagogue of Satan who say that they are Jews and are not, but are lying." As with the letter to the church in Smyrna (see 2:9), the language is hateful, polemical, pejorative, and dualistic in allying the synagogue with Satan against God and the Jesus-believers. Certainly the presence of such language in our Bible offers no sanction for contemporary Christians to speak about Jews—or anyone else—in these terms.

It is not clear whether there is an actual conflict between two groups or whether the author is drawing a contrast between them for other reasons. Given that there is no reference to slander (as in 2:9) or any other matter of doctrinal or confessional conflict, the latter option seems more convincing. The point of the contrast is to underline the faithful actions of Jesus- believers commended in verses 8 and 10.

John's criticism of the synagogue members seems to be, as in the letter to Smyrna, that they are faithless to their identity and heritage as God's people. As we noted in that letter, Jews in cities like Philadelphia participated in trade and commerce, gathered in the theater, held political office, spoke Greek, engaged in Greek education in the gymnasium, participated in actions that honored a range of elite figures from local city administrators to the emperor, promoted their own community's well-being with gifts, attracted Gentile sympathizers to synagogue communities, and celebrated Roman power. As far as John is concerned, these behaviors and practices show that Jews are too culturally accommodated as active participants in their first-century urban contexts and civic structures. He does not regard this as a faithful way to live. They are not faithful Jews in his view, and Jesus-believers should not have anything to do with or imitate these practices.

Accordingly, John borrows some Hebrew Bible language to announce judgment on them (3:9). The image of making them "bow down before your feet" appears in Hebrew Bible passages that depict God's coming victory (eschatology) in which the nations that have harassed Israel will submit to God (Isa 49:23; 60:14). But here the image is reversed. John's fantasy is that the synagogue will bow before the Jesus-believers and acknowledge their special place in God's victorious purposes.

In the meantime, the risen Christ will continue to guard their faithfulness (3:10). He will keep them safe through a coming time of "trial that is coming on the whole world." Unlike the claims of reading strategy 1 that believers will be taken out of the world's hardship in the rapture (discussed in chapter 1), the risen Christ promises to sustain them *through* it until he returns (3:11).

The letter concludes in 3:12 with several images of their participation in the completion of God's purposes. The first is the victor's "crown," or garland, won in athletic games and festivals. The second comprises becoming a permanent "pillar in the temple of my God," not a pillar of their society. The image might suggest a pillar that supports the roof of the temple or, more probably, it suggests a freestanding pillar that functions as a monument that honors a significant person or persons. Imitating this cultural practice, Revelation declares that faithful believers are honored by sharing in God's victory and presence. We should note that in the vision of the New Jerusalem in chapter 21 there is no temple in which to locate pillars (21:22). Clearly with these shifting images, John is not primarily concerned with consistency. The third image involves the inscribing of three names on the pillar. The names reveal that the ones honored belong to the victorious God, Christ, and the New Jerusalem.

The letter ends with the usual exhortation to "listen to what the Spirit is saying to the churches" (3:13).

## Laodicea (3:14-22)

The final church addressed is some 40 miles southeast of Philadelphia. The letter lacks any commendation (like the church in Sardis, 3:1-6) and is harshly critical of the church's complacency and high levels of assimilation to its urban context.

The exalted Christ in 3:14 presents himself as the "Amen," or "the faithful and true witness," to God's purposes. He has this sta-

46

tus of being a faithful witness because he was, like the figure of wisdom described in Prov 8:22-31, present with God in the beginning as "the origin of God's creation." He speaks of what he knows.

His words to the church in verses 15-16 condemn the church for being "lukewarm," "neither cold nor hot." After the presentation of the exalted Christ as the faithful witness, the image of being "lukewarm" suggests a lack of witness and unfaithful or half-hearted living. The threat that "I am about to spit you out of my mouth" suggests imminent judgment unless the situation changes. The image of being lukewarm and spat out might derive from Laodicea's water supply that flowed over limestone cliffs and was unpleasant, warm, and smelled of sulfur.

The church's failing is intensified in that its self-perception is greatly at odds with that of the exalted Christ (3:17), "For you say, 'I am rich, I have prospered, and I need nothing.'" These terms suggest that at least some in the church have accumulated some wealth, perhaps from the use of particular skills or from trade involving textile processing. The verb "prospered" or "grown rich" is used in chapter 18 in the condemnation of Rome and its worldwide empire. It especially refers to commercial activity associated with merchants (18:3, 15, 19). This declaration suggests considerable participation in and benefit from societal involvement.

The exalted Christ offers a different evaluation that challenges their complacency and material prosperity and lays bare their empty and misguided existence: "you are wretched, pitiable, poor, blind, and naked" (3:17). Then with love he calls them to repent (3:19) by using four metaphors.

The first redefines the metaphors of "buying" and "rich" (3:17-18). They are to invest in active and lived commitment to Christ. The second metaphor urges them to acquire "white robes," an image used in the letter to Sardis in 3:4 to denote victorious participation in the completion of God's purposes (3:5), worship (4:4), loyalty to God (6:11), allegiance to the exalted Christ (7:9, 13-14), and purity (19:14). To do so means an end to their societal accommodation and consuming economic activity. The third image offers "salve to anoint your eyes so that you may see" (3:18). This image refers to abandoning their inaccurate self-perception of 3:17a so as to gain insight into God's purposes, and discernment of a vastly different way of life (3:17b-19).

The fourth metaphor involves knocking on a door and, if invited in, a shared meal (3:20). This image invites them to respond positively to the letter's rebuke and to enjoy the blessing of divine presence and fellowship. Several letters use the image of eating (2:7, 17), contrasting the eating of idol-food with participation in the completion of God's purposes. It is a common image in the biblical tradition for the final inclusion of all people in God's plans. For example, we have this marvelous vision from Isaiah:

> On this mountain the LORD of hosts will make for all peoples
>> a feast of rich food, a feast of well-aged wines,
>> of rich food filled with marrow, of well-aged wines strained
>>> clear.
> And he will destroy on this mountain
>> the shroud that is cast over all peoples,
>> the sheet that is spread over all nations;
>> he will swallow up death forever.
> Then the Lord GOD will wipe away the tears from all faces,
>> and the disgrace of his people he will take away from all the
>>> earth,
>> for the LORD has spoken.
> It will be said on that day,
>> Lo, this is our God; we have waited for him, so that he might
>>> save us.
> This is the LORD for whom we have waited;
>> let us be glad and rejoice in his salvation. (25:6-9)

Another image follows that underlines the eschatological blessing that awaits them if they repent and live faithfully ("conquer"). "I will give a place with me on my throne, just as I myself conquered and sat down with my Father on his throne" (3:21). The throne image assures them that they will participate in the completion of God's rule just as was promised to the church in Thyatira if it repents and distances itself from cultural involvement (2:26b-27). The letter concludes with an exhortation to "listen to what the Spirit is saying to the churches" (3:22).

## Conclusion

The letters have revealed that cultural accommodation to and participation in the religiously intertwined, socioeconomic, and political structures and practices of these cities in the Roman province of Asia (Turkey) is dangerous. It involves honoring idols and various deities and representatives of Roman power. Participation in such activities and practices, is, for John, at odds with faithful commitment to God. Not all Jesus-believers in the cities, though, think the same way. This condemnation—consistently repeated through the seven letters in these two chapters—raises an important question: why is such participation so dangerous? The rest of Revelation is very concerned with this question and will reveal a number of answers.

## Study Questions

1. What, according to John, is going on in each of the churches addressed: Thyatira, Sardis, Philadelphia, and Laodicea? Do their strengths and weaknesses resemble your own church's life in any way?

2. What do you think about the presentation of Jezebel in the letter to the church in Thyatira (2:18-29)? John clearly despises her. How would you evaluate her way of, and possible rationale for, negotiating Roman culture?

3. Do we as readers have more in common with Jezebel's engagement with her culture than John's passionate opposition to it?

4. What do you think of the style or tone of the way John addresses the seven churches in these two chapters? If John were writing to your church and did so in the style of these letters, would you publish it, as is, in your church newsletter or website? Or would you want to edit it? How and why?

CHAPTER 5

# Revelation Reveals True Worship (Rev 4–5)

We have seen a consistent theme running through the seven letters to the seven churches. John is opposed to what he considers to be too great an involvement by Jesus-believers in their urban societies with their complex mix of religion, economics, social structures, and politics. They should have nothing to do with food offered to idols or with images and idols in general. He commends them when he observes some separation and distance but more often than not he rebukes them for being too cozy with their societies. The letters to the seven churches in chapters 2 and 3 reveal that cultural accommodation is dangerous.

But why is it so dangerous? Jezebel does not think it is dangerous to eat food offered to idols nor to be involved in a society where honoring idols and images is pervasive. Nor do the "Balaamites" or the Nicolaitans. They do not think that Jesus-believers need to distance themselves from honoring idols and images with prayers, offerings, sacrifices, games, feasts, and other gatherings that pervaded all activities of daily life. They and their numerous followers do not think that these and other commercial activities endanger Jesus-believers. Perhaps they have been influenced by Paul's arguments that "no idol in the world really exists," that "there is no God but one," and that "for us there is one God, the Father" (1 Cor 8:4-6). Perhaps they have been influenced by biblical figures who cooperated with and benefited from imperial power. Perhaps they see accommodation as necessary, for pragmatic or pastoral reasons.

John addresses a situation of conflict and various practices and opinions over this matter. So having asserted his foundational point that cultural accommodation is dangerous, he now sets about revealing in the rest of Revelation *why* it is dangerous. In chapters 4–5, he argues that it betrays the true worship of God and Jesus.

Chapters 4–5 consist of a second vision. The focus of the vision is heavenly worship of God (ch. 4) and the Lamb, Jesus (ch. 5). These chapters reveal the true worship that is already underway in the heavens in contrast to what John thinks is the false worship in which Jesus-believers are involved in civic festivals and idolatry in their cities. John's strategy is to disqualify participation in all other worship activity by revealing the true worship of God. How can Jesus-believers engage in any other worship activity? How can Jesus-believers be present when images are honored in any way in their cities, when only God and Jesus are worthy to receive worship (4:11; 5:12)? If only they could "see" this true worship, they would know to avoid false worship.

Further, at the center of the vision of the worship of God is God's throne, the place of power (4:2). One way of understanding apocalyptic thinking that pervades an apocalypse like Revelation is to recognize its central question: to whom does the sovereignty of the world belong? John's proclamation is that God is sovereign. God is in control of this world and the churches addressed in chapters 2–3. God alone deserves their worship. In comparison, the honoring of various divine and imperial figures in the cities is illusory and false. Despite all appearances and claims to the contrary, they are not in control. The world does not belong to them. They do not rule the world. They do not merit honoring activities. The chapters reveal that such worship belongs only to God and Jesus. Believers cannot be involved in both sorts of worship.

The language in these chapters is vivid and metaphorical. It does not claim to offer a photograph of heaven. Rather, like a music video, the images are constantly moving and blurring into one another, creating a collage of impressions. The word *like*, which occurs multiple times (4:1, 3, 6-7), contributes significantly to the mystical quality of the scene. Commonly the images are drawn from the Hebrew Scriptures and assume that we will automatically know what they mean. But, ironically, the images also reflect practices of honoring the emperor. John imitates and employs the very practices he is resisting.

## Revelation 4: Worship of God the Creator

John looks up to see "in heaven a door stood open" (4:1). This phrase echoes Ezek 1:1 and again associates John with the prophets, emphasizing his authority. The "open door" also creates the expectation of a revelation of God's purposes. The same voice who addressed John in Rev 1:10-11, the risen Christ, invites him into the heavens to "show you what must take place after this" (4:1). This phrase does not promise predictions of future, end-time events, but simply refers to further revelations after the ascent into the heavens. Tours of the heavens are common in apocalyptic literature (2 Cor 12; 1 Enoch 1–36; 2 Enoch).

In heaven, attention focuses on the "one seated on the throne" (4:2). The image is a common one for God in the Hebrew Bible (Pss 45:6; 47:8; Isa 6:1; Ezek 1:26). It recurs regularly through Revelation (4:9-10; 5:1, 7, 13; 6:16; 7:10, 15; 19:4; 21:5). It is an image of God's power, control, and authority at work in the world. The scene reveals the one who *really* rules the world, whatever the cities' leaders and activities claimed.

The description of the heavenly throne room comprises five elements.

First there are colors of precious stones that evoke the splendor and magnificence of God, "jasper" (variously translucent, yellow, red, or green), "carnelian," (red) and "a rainbow that looks like an emerald" (a spectrum of colors in which green dominates, 4:3). Second, the rainbow recalls the story of Noah and the display of God's mercy. Having punished human sin, God declares that never again will there be "a flood to destroy the earth." God set the rainbow in the sky as "a sign of the covenant" that God makes to be merciful (Gen 9:13). The heavenly worship celebrates God's merciful faithfulness.

Third, the "flashes of lightning, and rumblings and peals of thunder" (4:5) suggest God's power and presence revealed in creation and storms (Ps 18:7-16). It also evokes God's self-revelation to Moses in the sounds and sights of Mount Sinai in the making of the covenant with Israel and the giving of the Ten Commandments (Exod 19:16-25). Thunder and lightning were also associated with Zeus or Jupiter, but Revelation does not find him in the heavens. Fourth, the "seven flaming torches," interpreted as "the seven spirits of God," suggest God's activity in the world (compare 1:4).

And fifth, "in front of the throne there is something like a sea of glass, like crystal" (4:6). In the biblical traditions, the sea is commonly understood as a threatening and dangerous place that God subdued and put in its place in creation (Gen 1:7; see Ps 69). At the throne, God's power establishes something gloriously beautiful "like a sea of glass, like crystal." God is presented as splendid, merciful, powerful, present, self-disclosing, and in control.

"Around the throne" are two groups, "twenty-four elders" who, with their thrones, share in God's rule (4:4), and "four living creatures" (4:6-8). Who the "twenty-four elders" are is not entirely clear. Are they angels, or saints, or the twelve apostles and twelve patriarchs? Do they represent the totality of God's people (all people), both Jew and Gentile? They appear regularly through Revelation and perform two functions. They worship God (4:10; 11:16; 19:4) and the exalted Christ, the Lamb (5:8, 11), and they explain things to John (5:5; 7:13).

The four living creatures evoke the visions of Ezekiel and Isaiah (Isa 6; Ezek 1:5-22). They are "like" a lion, an ox, a human being, and an eagle, suggesting that they might represent all creation (wild and domestic animals, humans, and birds), though there is no representative from the sea. "Full of eyes" (4:6), they see everything and thereby guard God's throne; "without ceasing" (4:8), they praise God. Their hymn celebrates God as "high and lofty" (Isa 6:1), as "holy" (totally committed to serving God's purposes), all-powerful ("almighty"), and everlasting (4:8-9). The twenty-four elders and the four living creatures spur each other on in worship (4:9-10). The twenty-four elders honor God by falling down and "[casting] their crowns before the throne," a practice employed by kings and princes in submitting to a more powerful ruler.

The second song sung by the elders reveals why God is "worthy... / to receive glory and honor and power" from all beings and creation (4:11). The reason is given in a clause beginning with "for": "for you created all things, / and by your will they existed and were created" (4:11). God is celebrated as creator. God's will brings creation into being. This matters because as the maker of all things, God has sovereignty over them. As the psalmist declares, "The earth is the LORD's and all that is in it" (Ps 24:1).

Such a claim, though, is not self-evident to some or even many members of the churches in the seven cities in the Roman province of Asia (Turkey) addressed in chapters 2–3. Their world is dominated by various gods and goddesses—like Artemis in Ephesus and Thyatira, or Zeus and Cybele in Smyrna, or Zeus and Asclepius in Pergamum, or Artemis and Cybele in Sardis, who claimed to be the source of blessing and life. And as Asia was a Roman province, imperial temples, images, personnel, and festivals celebrated Rome and its emperors as being chosen by the gods to manifest their sovereignty, power, and will among humans. Rome's was a proprietary empire in which everything on the earth and in the sea belonged to the emperor. Provincial government, taxation, and requisitions of supplies for the army were three ways of demonstrating Rome's ownership of "the earth... and all that is in it."

The address to God in verse 11 as "our Lord and God" evokes and contests these claims. The writer Suetonius indicates that this very same address "our Lord and God" was associated with the emperor Domitian, emperor from 81–96 C.E. in the time span when Revelation was probably written (Suetonius, *Domitian*, 13.2; Dio Cassius, 67.4.7). Revelation imitates and disputes this claim. Only one is worthy to be so identified and only one is to be worshiped as creator. All other worship is illegitimate and invalid. Believers should not participate in it.

## Revelation 5: Worship of the Redeemer

The vision of God as the one worthy to receive worship as the sovereign creator of all things becomes a vision of the exalted Christ in chapter 5. He too is worthy to receive worship. He is the redeemer who carries out God's saving purposes. The assumption of this claim is that the world viewed as blessed by various gods and rulers and under Roman control is a sinful claim from which the world needs setting free.

The focus initially falls on a "scroll" in "the right hand of the one seated on the throne" (5:1). Such precise attention to God's right hand is at odds with the mysterious and glorious visionary presentation of God in chapter 4. Again the language is metaphorical and evocative, not literal. The right hand represents God's authority and power (1:16). The scroll is God's possession. It is sealed to guarantee its legitimacy and to preserve it only for those worthy to read it. It outlines God's purposes for redemptive justice as chapters 6–8 will show.

The writing down of God's purposes on a scroll is common in prophetic and apocalyptic writings. Ezekiel is given a scroll, also written "on the front and on the back," full of "lamentations and mourning and woe" (Ezek 2:10). Daniel is ordered to keep his book "sealed until the time of the end" (Dan 12:4).

An angel raises the question, "Who is worthy to open the scroll and break its seals?" The seals need to be broken so as to reveal its contents and to carry them out (5:2). No one in all creation ("in heaven or on earth or under the earth") is found worthy to do so (5:3), and John weeps that without an agent God's purposes will go unknown and unaccomplished (5:4).

An elder intervenes with the startling reassurance that there is one who is worthy (5:5). The elder introduces this worthy figure first in terms of ruling power and then, surprisingly, in terms of vulnerable suffering. The elder first identifies him as "the Lion of the tribe of Judah, the Root of David, [who] has conquered" (5:5). The image of a lion is one of ruling power. It comes from Jacob, who calls his son Judah a lion in that a king, a ruler, would come from his line (Gen 49:9-10). The "Root of David" refers to the descendants of King David to whom God also promised a line of kings forever (2 Sam 7; Ps 89:1-4) that would rule over all the nations (Ps 72:1-11).

But strangely, John does not see a lion. This image of ruling power immediately morphs into one of vulnerable suffering. John sees "a Lamb standing as if it had been slaughtered" (5:6). There are paradoxes aplenty. The lion is a lamb. The Lamb appears to have been slaughtered but is alive. Power is vulnerability. Yet it is standing, has "seven horns," a symbol of power (see Deut 33:17), and "seven eyes," a symbol of all knowledge (5:6).

The "slaughtered lamb" is Revelation's central image for Jesus. The biblical tradition associates lambs with daily temple sacrifices for sin (Exod 29:38-42), with the liberation of the people from Egypt at Passover where the lambs protected and identified the people rather than cleansing them from sin (Exod 12), and with the suffering servant who absorbs imperial violence on behalf of the people (Isa 53:4-12). What sort of lamb is the exalted Christ?

Interestingly, Revelation uses the verb "slaughtered" or "slain" not in relation to sacrifice but in relation to violent death (Rev 6:4; 13:3; 18:24, author's translation). This use defines the exalted Christ as the "slain lamb" in that he has suffered the violence of Roman power in his crucifixion. Jesus did not use violence to resist imperial violence but absorbed its violence, even to death, while he entrusted himself to God's life-giving power. That he is "standing" signifies God's overcoming of imperial power by faithfully raising him from the dead and exalting him into the heavens. Rome could not keep him dead.

This description of the exalted Christ as "slain but standing" is important because it reveals to Revelation's readers the violence of the Roman system. It reveals that the world to which some or many of the Jesus-believers in the seven cities were happily accommodated violently rejected Jesus, the agent of God's purposes. But it also reveals that God sided with Jesus, not Rome, in raising Jesus from the dead. Roman power and violence are not ultimate; they do not have the last word. God's life-giving actions prevail. This imperial world is, then, not a world in which Jesus-believers can readily be at home. And they certainly cannot fool themselves that participating in civic and association rituals of worship that involve idols, images, offerings, prayers, and meals is harmless, that religion and politics do not mix, that idols do not demand allegiance.

The Lamb takes the scroll from God, thereby becoming the agent of God's purposes (5:7). He will accomplish what the scroll declares. His taking of the scroll brings further worship from the continually worshiping, harp-playing, incense-bearing, prayer-offering, twenty-four elders and four creatures (5:8-9). They sing a "new song" (5:9), a term that the Hebrew Bible uses to celebrate new acts of God's delivering power from Babylonian exile (Ps 40:3; Isa 42:10).

As with the song in 4:11 that declares why God the creator is worthy to receive worship, this song—also with a clause beginning with "for"—declares why the Lamb is worthy to "take the scroll / and to open its seals, / for you were slaughtered and by your blood you ransomed for God / saints from every tribe" (5:9). The Lamb is worthy because in his violent death ("slaughtered," "blood") he has ransomed a worldwide people committed to God's purposes in the midst of Roman and civic power. John's emphasis is not on individuals but on forming communities who serve God as a "kingdom" or "empire," as "priests" in offering worship, and who share in God's rule on earth. In taking the scrolls and breaking the seals, the Lamb enacts God's will to establish God's sovereign purposes throughout God's world, beginning with this people.

Is this a vision of the future when God's purposes are established in full? Or does it refer to the present? The answer is probably both. God has always been about forming a people to carry out God's purposes. The language in 5:10 of being a "kingdom and priests" echoes God's covenant with Israel at Mt. Sinai to be "a priestly kingdom and a holy nation" (Exod 19:6). Revelation has used similar language in 1:6 to describe the churches in relation to Jesus' death. It is an identity and role that already applies to the churches. Here the language of "serving God" challenges those in the churches that John thinks are compromised in their loyalty through participation in gatherings that involve honoring idols. Yet there is also a future dimension. In the final visions in Revelation of God's fully established will, people reign with the Lamb and thereby participate in the complete establishment of God's sovereign purposes (20:4-6).

More and more figures—angels, the living creatures, and the elders—join in celebrating the worthiness of "the Lamb that was slaughtered" (5:11-14). The term "myriads" indicates a large but undefined number of these heavenly figures. They are joined by "every creature in heaven and on earth and under the earth and in the sea, and all that is in them" in praising both God ("the one seated on the throne") and the Lamb (5:13).

58

This reference to "every creature" (5:13) is a stunning vision of all creation, including all people, acknowledging their creator and savior in worship. It sits in some tension with some of the material we have read in the previous chapters. We have seen, for example, in the letters to the churches that John's vision is uncompromising in its demand for exclusive loyalty to God. He does not make space for diversity of practices and thinking and seems quite sure as to who is in and who is out of God's purposes. Yet now he envisions all people and all creation in harmonious relationship with their creator and redeemer.

# A Final Irony

There is a further ironic dimension of these worship scenes in chapters 4–5 that we should note. John has been adamant in chapters 2–3 that Jesus-believers are not to participate in the daily honoring of the gods and goddesses and the imperial powers that pervade the cities in which they live and seek to support themselves. He wants an end to such accommodation and a separation from such activity because he regards it to be at odds with loyalty to God. His vision of heavenly worship in chapters 4–5 reveals true worship, the worship of God and the exalted Christ. With such a vision before them, how can Jesus-believers continue to participate in such civic honoring? How can they think it is powerless and inconsequential? The dramatic vision, the revelation of this true worship and of God and the Lamb as the only ones worthy of worship, is to persuade the churches to cease from such participation.

Yet there are some striking similarities between this vision of exclusive worship for God, and the ways in which Roman emperors were honored, whether in Rome or in traveling throughout the empire. The imperial court, like this depiction of the heavenly court, was a dazzling display of wealth, power, and status. Roman emperors were continually addressed and accompanied by figures like the twenty-four elders, folks who were advisors, "friends," envoys from provincial cities, and slaves. Emperors were honored with the offering of sacrifices and incense. They were greeted with processions and the offering of crowns. They were the subject and object of hymns of praise and shouts of acclamation. Subordinates greeted them by ascribing titles to them and by prostrating themselves before them. That is, all the behaviors we see in chapters 4–5 that honor God and the Lamb resemble the ways people honored emperors and other imperial officials.

This is a significant irony. Like bumper stickers that declare "waging war for peace," John opposes imperial ways, even while he imitates them in presenting his vision of true worship and trying to persuade Jesus-believers to distance themselves from imperial society. The irony suggests that John's demand for exclusive loyalty to God is more easily made than it is carried out.

## Study Questions

1. Revelation 4 and 5 are rich chapters that dramatically describe heavenly worship. What do you find most interesting about this description? What do you think of the similarity between John's vision of heavenly worship and practices of worshiping the emperor? Does this similarity compromise John's call for Jesus-followers to distance themselves from the Roman Empire?

2. Our tradition includes other descriptions or visions of worshiping God. Read, for example, Isaiah 6:1-5 and Ezekiel 1. Why do we worship God? What kind of worship is most true for you?

3. For John, worship is political; the decision to worship God means not worshiping any other in any way (no involvement in celebrations involving idols or food offered to idols, and so on). In what ways might we think about our worship as being political? What consequences might that have?

CHAPTER 6

# Revelation Reveals That Judgment Is Taking Place Now (Rev 6:1–8:5)

Revelation 6–8 build on the worship scenes of chapters 4–5 in that they narrate the opening of the seals on the scroll that Jesus the Lamb has taken in his hand from God. In these chapters John provides another reason why Jesus-believers in the seven cities in the Roman province of Asia (Turkey) should not eat food offered to idols and should not participate in their image- and idol-rich urban contexts as though these were harmless activities.

In chapters 4–5 he revealed that true worship of God is exclusive since only God the creator and Jesus the Lamb (who carries out God's purposes) are worthy of worship. There is no room for involvement in honoring images and idols in civic activities. In chapters 6–8, he reveals another reason for nonparticipation in such activity and for societal distance. His new revelation is that their daily world, under Roman control and shaped by various gods and goddesses, is under God's judgment. This imperial world in which they are active participants and to which they are overaccommodated is not as God wants it to be.

There are two key parts to this revelation. First, this revelation of the Roman imperial world under God's judgment concerns the present. Chapters 6–8 do not predict some future time. They concern God's judgment that is under way already, in the present. And second, the chapters reveal that this judgment does not take place by God hurling down thunderbolts from heaven. Rather, God's judgment is evident in the self-destructive ways in which the Roman imperial world organizes and conducts itself.

This claim that the Roman Empire was under God's judgment was of course not obvious to everyone in the seven churches, let alone in their cities. There were various assessments of the Roman Empire. Jezebel's verdict seems to have been quite positive. Roman elites and their allies in provincial cities generally saw Rome as being chosen by the gods to manifest their will and purposes. The Jewish writer Josephus, who lived at the same time as Revelation was written, has one of his characters declare God's sanction for the Roman empire, "for without God's aid so vast an empire could never have been built up" (*Jewish War* 2.390-91). Yet while the writer of 2 Esdras—found in the collection of writings we know as the Apocrypha—can recognize that God made Rome to rule in the world (2 Esd 11:39), he also declares God's judgment on Rome's empire:

> You have held sway over the world with great terror, and over all the earth with grievous oppression;...for you have oppressed the meek and injured the peaceable;...Your insolence has come up before the Most High, and your pride to the Mighty One....Therefore you, eagle, will surely disappear,...so that the whole earth, freed from your violence, may be refreshed and relieved, and may hope for the judgment and mercy of him who made it. (2 Esd 11:40-46)

Revelation's view is much more akin to this latter perspective.

## Opening the Seals: Revealing God's Purposes (Chapter 6)

Crucial for chapters 6–8 is the scroll that the Lamb had taken from God in 5:7. Chapter 5 celebrated the Lamb's identity as the agent of God's purposes; he is the one who is worthy to take the scroll and unseal the scrolls' seven seals (5:4-5). That is, God's purposes are revealed through Jesus. They are not revealed through the emperor, as imperial ideology claimed, and they are not revealed through the gods and goddesses like Zeus, Asclepius, and Artemis that the cities claimed and honored, festivities in which some Jesus-believers participated.

But while chapter 5 has revealed Jesus' role, it has not revealed God's judgments. The seals wait to be opened. Chapters 6–8 narrate Jesus' opening of the seals and reveal God's purposes at work in the world of the seven churches.

**First Seal (6:1-2)**

In verse 1, the Lamb (the exalted Christ crucified and risen) opens the first seal. One of the four living creatures cries "Come!" and John sees the first of four different-colored horses that will appear as each of the first four seals is opened. The four scenes do not show the horses coming from God. They represent—and interpret—realities already present in the world.

This famous vision of "the four horsemen of the Apocalypse" borrows the images of colored horses from Zech 6:1-5. There they represent the Persian Empire, whose power is contained within and by God's rule. Here they depict aspects of Rome's empire, also contained within God's sovereignty. The seals do not predict events that will happen but reveal God's purposes already active in the present, Roman-ruled world through the consequences of its ruling ways.

The "white horse" signifies victory or conquest. "White" is the color of victory (2:17; 3:5). It also indicates horses that were valued by high-ranking officers. The bow evokes the mounted archers of the army of the Parthians, Rome's main rival to the east. The crown is the wreath of victory. Twice the verb *conquers* emphasizes conquest.

This seal is not a prediction of future events as much as it is an interpretation of things happening already in the present. It reveals the norm of imperial ways and politics that wherever empires assert their dominating power to further their own interests, secure resources, and oppress people, inevitably some will contest and resist that power. Conflict and struggle are a certainty, whether with another empire like Parthia or from within Rome's empire, involving local peoples like the Judeans who revolted in 66–70 C.E. Rome's empire had been gained and secured by both conquest and alliance building. Asia had become part of the empire by treaty several centuries previously in 133 B.C.E. Recent events in Judea from 66–70 C.E., however, showed that some local peoples were willing to revolt. Roman armies had defeated Jerusalem and destroyed its temple in 70 C.E. Conflict was inevitable as was Rome's readiness to use its military power to ensure compliance and submission.

The first seal reveals that such conquest and struggle, though not caused by God, fall within God's purview and enact God's purposes of justice and judgment. The world does not need God's thunderbolts to execute God's judgment. Judgment is at work in the "normal," destructive, and oppressive struggle for power among nations.

## Second Seal (6:3-4)

The scenario involving the second seal largely repeats the scenario and message of the first one. Repetition underlines the point. A red horse, the color of bloodshed, appears whose "rider was permitted to take peace from the earth." The references to "slaughter" and "a great sword" indicate war and bloodshed.

Again the scene does not predict a future event as much as it interprets that constant of human experience, war, in the context of God's purposes. It reveals that a world in which the violence and bloodshed of war dominates is a world that destroys itself. It reveals that God's judgment is already experienced in such activity in which humans and nations choose to pursue war to further their own purposes, rather than choosing ways of peace and mutual coexistence.

## Third Seal (6:5-6)

War is often a struggle for land and human and material resources. In the ancient world, food resources, just as energy sources and access to water today, were matters of power. War often leads to famine and hardship.

On the opening of this third seal, "a black horse" appears as a symbol of death, associated here with food shortages. The reason for death is explained by the scales or "yoke" that the rider holds and by the voice that cries, "A quart of wheat for a day's pay, and three quarts of barley for a day's pay, but do not damage the olive oil and the wine!" The focus has moved from the political and military struggles of the first two seals to economic and commercial practices, particularly food supply. Political disputes and war frequently disrupt food supply and cause widespread hardship for common folks. The prices for the quantities of wheat and barley—staples for many folks—are high, indicating a food shortage, if not famine. The protection for olive oil and wine suggests some calculation in disrupting some food supply, but not all.

The scene continues to offer a vignette of the consequences of life ordered on earth contrary to God's purposes. It reveals that when rulers choose political and military conflicts, economic disruption is inevitable. Food supply is damaged. Many people in the ancient world experienced daily food shortages while elites who benefited from imperial power, wealth, and status usually enjoyed abundance. The scene reveals that the world implodes under the inequities of this destructive system. These consequences are God's judgment already active in its midst.

## Fourth Seal (6:7-8)

The fourth seal reveals a "pale green horse," the color of sickness and decaying flesh. Its rider is identified as death, followed by Hades, the dwelling place of the dead. They are given—presumably by God—"authority over a fourth of the earth," an indication of power that is also limited by God's greater sovereignty. They exercise this authority "with sword, famine, and pestilence, and . . . wild animals" (6:8). These are the consequences not just of war but of the ways that the Roman Empire organized the world. The scene reveals the world imploding as a result of wrong choices and an unjust system that benefits a few but brings great distress to many. It reveals that God's judgment is being worked out in the present imperial world in which human freedom is asserted in abusive and destructive ways.

## Fifth Seal (6:9-11)

The fifth and sixth seals move from earth to heaven. The focus remains on revealing the destructive impact of imperial rule on those living on the earth. With the fifth seal, victims of imperial injustice cry out for God to take revenge (6:10). This vision of martyrs begging for divine intervention names a question emerging from the first four scenes. Those previous scenes have revealed God's judgment to be at work in the destructive actions and structures of Rome's empire in which the seven cities participate. But yet that world and its destructive and oppressive ways continue.

Why doesn't God act decisively to end such injustice? Does God not care? Is God aloof and indifferent to human suffering? Is God powerless before it and unable to do anything about it? Such are the issues that the martyrs' cry engages: "Sovereign Lord, holy and true, how long will it be before you judge and avenge our blood on the inhabitants of the earth?" (6:10). The martyrs call for God's revenge on God's enemies. The language of "how long" is found in lament psalms where the psalmist impatiently complains or whines about God's apparent lack of concern for or inability to do anything about circumstances of suffering (Pss 13:1-2; 74:9-10; 80:3-19; 82:2-5; 94:1-7). Why does God not intervene?

The questioners are Jesus-believers or martyrs who are presented as having been "slaughtered" by imperial violence as a result of their commitment and testimony to "the word of God." The verb *slaughtered*, or *slain*, allies them with the Lamb who was also slain by imperial power (5:6). Many interpreters have suggested that the scene refers to persecutions of Jesus-believers that have happened or are about to happen. But we must remember it is a vision, not a report or a prediction. We have no evidence for empire-wide, first-century, capital persecution of believers who refused to honor the emperor. We do have evidence for isolated conflicts such as the emperor Nero's outburst in the 60s in Rome and that referred to by Governor Pliny in his correspondence with the emperor Trajan in the early second century in the province of Bithynia-Pontus. These outbursts were not empire-wide or sustained over long periods. And anyway, the vision in 6:9-11 focuses less on how they died and more on the injustice that remains to be addressed.

It seems more helpful to understand the scene as revealing another dynamic that comes into play when imperial power is asserted. *In John's presentation*, the assertion of imperial power means conflict with God's people because such power is fundamentally at odds with God's purposes. John could appeal to various Hebrew Bible narratives that describe conflicts in which God's people suffered even to death and in which God's deliverance seemed to be delayed before it was experienced: slavery in Egypt (Exod 1–5), life in exile under Assyrian and Babylonian power in the eighth through sixth centuries B.C.E. (the setting for the stories of Dan 1–6), the assault of the Seleucid ruler Antiochus Epiphanes in the 160s B.C.E. (1 Macc 1–2; Daniel).

Jezebel, though, would say by way of response that this is a simplistic analysis. She would point to biblical traditions in which God's people cooperated with imperial power such as Joseph in Egypt (Gen 37, 39–47) or Jeremiah's advice to the exiles to settle into life in Babylonian exile (Jer 29). She could also note examples in which God uses imperial powers, such as God's commissioning of the Persian ruler Cyrus to let the people return from Babylonian exile to their own land (Isa 44:24–45:1-8). John's concern, of course, is that there is already too much accommodation. He seeks to reveal the fundamental incompatibility between the commitments of the seven churches and the imperial world in which they live.

In response, the martyrs are "told to rest a little longer, until the number would be complete" (6:11). The time of the completion of God's purposes is not yet. Injustice will continue but the martyrs are assured that there will be such a time when God's judgment is completed and God's justice established (6:11). Will that mean revenge, or will all God's enemies be drawn into creation's free and all-inclusive worship of its creator God (5:13)?

## Sixth Seal (6:12-17)

The opening of the sixth seal reveals a terrible scene of cosmic disintegration. There are earthquakes, dramatic changes to sun and moon, falling stars (nothing romantic about them!), the rolling up of the sky-dome, the transplanting of mountains and islands (6:12-14). We must remember that no actual planets or people were damaged in the production of Revelation. We are reading a description of a vision, not watching video to accompany a news report.

Is this scene the end of the world as we know it? Is this the "wrath of the Lamb" (6:16) let loose?

It seems not. First, this cosmic chaos, the reversal of creation, does not destroy human beings. "Then the kings of the earth and

67

the magnates and the generals and the rich and the powerful, and everyone, slave and free, hid in the caves and among the rocks" (6:15). Seven human groups are involved, the number seven denoting *all* humans. The powerful, wealthy, and high-status, the first five, are emphasized, but the phrase "slave and free" is all inclusive. Slaves were human victims of the assertion of imperial power; the Roman Empire could not function without them.

And second, this cosmic disruption announces the coming of "the great day of their wrath." It precedes and anticipates that day. The feature of that day will be that no one will be "able to stand" (6:17).

So what does the scene reveal about the "wrath of the Lamb"? The Lamb is the exalted Christ introduced in 1:5 as the one "who loves us and freed us from our sins." His redeeming work (6:9) displays the love of God by absorbing imperial violence. As we noted when the Lamb was introduced in 5:6 as "standing as if it had been slaughtered," it is a paradoxical figure. The very phrase "wrath of the Lamb" is a paradox. What does the wrath of the one "who loves us" look like? Is it the violent revenge the martyrs under the altar demand, or, as is more likely, is it a display of cautioning love?

**The Seventh Seal? Not Yet (7:1-17)**

The sequence of the opening of seals is interrupted. The seventh seal will be opened in chapter 8. Before then, chapter 7 offers two scenes of encouragement and consolation. The scenes relieve the intensely disturbing sequence of the first four scenes and address the cry for revenge against Rome uttered in 6:10. Significantly, they assure the Jesus-believers in the seven churches that judgment is not God's only activity in the present. God is also at work saving and protecting a people in the midst of this imperial world. This is the significance of the sealing that verses 3-4 describe.

John sees "four angels" who have responsibility for controlling the wind on the earth. Other angels have responsibility for natural forces in Revelation (14:18, fire; 16:5, water). The vision continues when another angel instructs them to restrain the wind until "we have marked the servants [slaves] of our God with a seal on their foreheads" (7:3). A seal was a branding that served primarily as a mark of ownership and possession, as well as of legal guarantee. Animals and slaves were "sealed" or branded. Kings sealed and thereby guaranteed a command or edict with a signet ring (Esth 8:8, 10; Dan 6:17). Ezekiel was commanded to put a mark on the foreheads of those who were troubled by the "abominations" committed in Jerusalem (Ezek 9:4). The sealing of the "slaves of our God...on their foreheads" depicts a group of people who belong to God.

What is the seal and who are the people? They are numbered in verse 4 as "one hundred and forty-four thousand, sealed out of every tribe of the people of Israel." Verses 5-8 catalog twelve from each of twelve tribes.

These verses raise many questions. Who are these people? Who are God's slaves or servants (7:3)? Is the number 144,000 literal or symbolic? If the former, it represents a tiny group. If the latter, it represents both a very large number and all people. The number twelve indicates completeness, so twelve times twelve depicts complete completeness or an innumerable number. How is "Israel" to be understood? If it is understood literally, they are faithful Jews. If it is understood to represent the people of God, then they could be Jesus-believers, or a combination of both Jesus-believers and Jews. If they are Jesus-believers, the seal on their foreheads (a symbol and not a literal mark) could represent baptism or the presence of the Spirit, which indicate belonging to the people of God.

There are many possibilities here and every one of these questions is hard to answer. However the specifics are identified, some very important general affirmations emerge. Certainly, the vision indicates God's sustaining presence with anyone who lives in a world out of shape. Certainly, the vision assures that God's presence in the midst of a broken and unjust world is as much for saving as it is for judging. And certainly, in the light of the vision in 5:13 of "every creature" caught up in the worship of God, the vision assures us of the vast and inclusive, all-encompassing scope of God's merciful presence. This vision leaves no room for stingy grace.

## Heavenly Worship (7:9-17)

The second scene is another magnificent vision of worship. The scene resembles chapters 4–5 in many ways. There is an international, white-robed, "great multitude that no one could count, from every nation...tribes...peoples and languages," who worship God and the Lamb, to whom salvation, or rescue, belongs (7:9). Angels, the elders, and the four living creatures also worship (7:11-12).

An elder identifies those in white robes as those who have remained faithful to God through "the great ordeal" (7:14). This ordeal is John's term for the world he has been revealing in chapters 1–6. This Roman-ruled world, as experienced in the seven cities, is self-promoting in its displays of power; celebratory in its pervasive use of temples, images and idols; but experiencing God's judgment in its self-destructive ways. Those who are not sucked into this world's ways are vindicated as participants in the true and exclusive worship of God and the Lamb (7:15a) and as participants in the completion of God's just and life-giving purposes (7:15b-17). This is another warning to those in the churches against participating in anything to do with idols.

## The Seventh Seal (8:1-5)

If we were expecting that the sequence of the opening of the seals was leading to a dramatic conclusion, we will be disappointed by this scene. After the revelations of divine judgment, presence, and worship, suddenly "there was silence in heaven for about half an hour" (8:1).

Two things happen in this silence. First, an "angel with a golden censer" stands at the altar and offers "the prayers of all the saints" to God (8:3). The scene offers a description of "bells-and-smells" worship with incense, smoke, fire, and "peals of thunder, rumblings, flashes of lightning, and an earthquake," all indications of divine presence (8:5). This same action of offering prayers to God was part of the worship scene in 5:8. Its repetition provides assurance and encouragement for the believers of God's attentiveness to their situation.

The second event occurs in verse 2: "I saw the seven angels who stand before God, and seven trumpets were given to them." These

70

angels and their blowing of the trumpets form the basis for the cycle of visions in chapters 8–11. We will discuss these scenes in the next chapter.

## Study Questions

1. Review 6:1-8 and John's portrayal of judgment as taking place in his lifetime in the self-destructive ways in which the Roman Empire structured its world. This is a very controversial claim for John to make; obviously the elites of the empire did not see it this way. Do you see "judgment" taking place in our world in any way? If so, how? If not, how do you understand the notion of judgment?

2. How do you think about the notion of God judging the world? Does God do so? Is God always merciful to human beings? Do we condemn ourselves?

# CHAPTER 7

# Revelation Reveals That the World Has a Chance to Repent (Rev 8–11)

C hapt.ers 8–11 are disturbing chapters. While they present more scenes of judgment, they now serve as descriptions of devastating damage to creation and the destruction of people. Several scenes follow in which witnesses faithful to God's purposes suffer. Why the repetition of judgment scenes and why an emphasis on suffering?

In the six scenes associated with the opening of the seals in chapter 6, we saw that Revelation reveals judgment at work in Rome's world in the present. Those visions reveal that this judgment does not take the form of direct punishment. God is not hurling thunderbolts down from heaven. Rather, the visions reveal that judgment is at work in the destructive means and consequences of imperial power. They show a self-imploding world as God allows such powers and structures to exercise their self-seeking and destructive power.

In chapters 8–9, another sequence of seven judgment scenes follows. Each of the seven angels with trumpets, who appeared before God in 8:2, blows his trumpet. Each blowing of a trumpet announces and reveals a new judgment scene. The chapters do not progressively build a uniform and coherent scenario. There are contradictions. In 8:7 a third of the trees and all the green grass are burned up, but in 9:4 the locusts are not allowed to damage trees or grass. The scenes do not fit together neatly like pieces of a jigsaw puzzle. Rather, as with the first sequence of judgment scenes in chapter 6, the chapters are like a music video presenting a constantly changing set of images depicting judgment.

Many readers of Revelation rightly find these chapters disturbing, with their descriptions of various ecological and human disasters. A third of the earth is burned up, a third of the sea becomes blood, and a third of humankind dies (8:7, 9, 11; 9:18). This relentless violence is more intense than in chapter 6. There, a quarter of the earth is damaged (6:8). Here, in chapters 8–9, a third of the earth is damaged. It all seems too much, too over the top.

What sort of God does this or even allows it? Is God having a meltdown or a tantrum? Why more scenes of violence? Why another sequence of appalling depictions of destruction and judgment that wipe out a third of the earth and its inhabitants?

The shocking quality of the scenes has several functions. First, it reminds us that these are visions. They are scenes of imagination. They paint their scenes much larger than life. They are not visuals accompanying the daily newscast. They are not real-life photographs depicting actual events. Nowhere is God *actually* turning the sea into blood, destroying a third of the earth, or wiping out a third of the world's population. These are imagined scenes. We must not treat them as though they were photographs.

Second, as disturbing scenes with shock value, they get our attention. They add another dimension to the previous revelations involving "true" worship (chs. 4–5) and the self-destructive nature of the present imperial world (chs. 6–7). In chapters 8–11, Revelation continues to paint large the terrible destructiveness of a world out of sorts in order to get the attention of those in the churches who continue to participate in the idol- and image-infused life of their cities as though there is no problem. These extravagant scenes shout loud and clear that there is a problem according to John.

And third, the chapters indicate the specific response they want from accommodated Jesus-believers. After the sixth trumpet is blown, we read:

> The rest of humankind, who were not killed by these plagues, did not repent of the works of their hands or give up worshiping demons and idols of gold and silver and bronze and stone and wood, which cannot see or hear or walk. And they did not repent of their murders or their sorceries or their fornication or their thefts. (9:20-21)

The terrible sequence of horror scenes is supposed to provoke Jesus-believers to repent of their accommodated living. These

74

over-the-top visionary scenes are more warnings or cautions than final declarations. They create merciful opportunities for repentance rather than forecasting final judgment. They are supposed to have enough dramatic impact that Jesus-believers change their ways of behaving and thinking in the actual world. Jesus-believers are to change their orientation toward their urban contexts and distance themselves from social and economic involvements in these idol-pervasive civic contexts.

Another dimension of the chapters confirms the function of these scenes as warnings that urge repentance. There are significant similarities between five of these seven disasters and the plagues that God sends on Pharaoh, ruler of Egypt. These scenes recall the Exodus story and the role of the plagues in getting Pharaoh's attention and causing him to change his mind about setting free the Israelites from slavery.

In Exod 7–12, God has declared that the people will be freed from slavery in Egypt. Pharaoh, though, refuses to "let my people go." So God sends a disaster on the Egyptians, notably turning water into blood. After seven days, Pharaoh still refuses to free the people. God sends a plague of frogs. Again Pharaoh refuses. And so it happens eight more times. Several times God declares that the plague is happening so that "by this you [Pharaoh] shall know that I am the LORD" (Exod 7:17; see also 8:10). That is, the plagues were not intended to punish Pharaoh but to reveal God at work so that Pharaoh would change his behavior to do God's will.

The link between the story of Pharaoh in Exodus and these trumpet-induced plagues in Revelation 8–9 is crucial for understanding their function.

| Trumpets | Description | Plagues of Egypt |
|---|---|---|
| Rev 8:7 | Hail, fire, blood | Exod 9:13-15; seventh plague |
| Rev 8:8-9 | Sea into blood | Exod 7:14-25; first plague |
| Rev 8:10-11 | Water becomes bitter | Exod 7:14-25; first plague (?) |
| Rev 8:12 | Darkness | Exod 10:21-29; ninth plague |
| Rev 9:1-11 | Locusts | Exod 10:1-20; eighth plague |

The "trumpet" scenes in Revelation evoke these plagues from Exodus to underscore that Revelation 8–11 reveals God at work in the world of these late first-century Jesus-believers. God is, so John claims, seeking a change in ways of thinking and living. God graciously offers Jesus-believers a chance to repent. And second, these scenes reveal that just as God was at work in the circumstances of the Egyptian empire and eventually triumphed, so also God will triumph here in the midst of Rome's empire. Jesus-believers should therefore change their ways. They should distance themselves from a world whose self-destructive ways manifest God's judgment.

The series of imaginative and exaggerated scenes is organized around blowing trumpets. Trumpets got people's attention, warning them (Ezek 33:3-6), and signaling God's presence and activity among the people (Exod 19:16; 20:8). Trumpets were associated with worship (Pss 81:3; 150:3). They called people to battle (Judg 3:27; 6:34; 7:8). All of these functions are appropriate for Revelation's call to the Jesus-believers in the seven cities in Asia to be faithful in their worship of God and to struggle against the false and idolatrous worship that pervaded activities in their cities.

## The First Four Trumpets (8:1-13)

Chapter 8 describes scenes associated with the blowing of the first four trumpets. While each is briefly narrated, by contrast, the extent of their damage is great. Images of terrible destruction and extensive ecological damage pile up. We must remember that we are reading visions. Poetic descriptions are not descriptions of literal events.

The first trumpet releases a horrendous ecological disaster as "hail and fire, mixed with blood" descend on the earth. As a result, "a third of the earth was burned up, and a third of the trees were burned up, and all green grass was burned up" (8:7).

The second scene pictures massive damage on the sea (8:8-9). "Something like" a fiery mountain "was thrown into the sea. A third of the sea [becomes] blood, a third of the living creatures in the sea [die], and a third of the ships [are] destroyed" (8:8-9).

76

The third scene concerns a blazing star destroying the fresh water supply found in "a third of the rivers and...the springs of water" (8:10). The star is called "Wormwood," the name of a bitter-tasting plant. This bitter plant is an image of God's harsh and chastening actions with Israel in Jer 9:15 and 23:15 as God attempts to change the people's way of living. "A third of the waters became wormwood, and many died from the water, because it was made bitter" (8:11).

The fourth scene moves from earth into the heavens, to the sun, moon, and stars (8:12). The attention to these heavenly lights recalls the first and fourth days of creation as God divides light from darkness and sets the sun and moon in the sky (Gen 1:1-19). The striking of the sun, moon, and stars meant the loss of "a third of their light" (8:12).

Before the fifth angel blows its trumpet, an eagle alerts us to a new focus in the sequence. Whereas the first four trumpets depict God's judgment in terms of imagined but massive destruction in the natural and cosmic worlds, the eagle indicates that the next three trumpets concern "woe to the inhabitants of the earth" (8:13). The woe will come from demonic forces.

## The Fifth and Sixth Trumpets (Ch. 9)

The fifth scene describes an attack of locust-like demons. Verses 1-2 of chapter 9 describe their origins in "the bottomless pit," the domain of Satan (11:7; 20:1-3). A fallen star or angel unlocks this pit, releasing first smoke and then the locusts (9:3a). Given this devilish origin, we might expect them to attack Jesus-believers. But believers are not their targets, and their role is closely limited by God.

Verses 3b-6 describe their role among "the inhabitants of the earth" (8:13). The locusts are not to damage grass or trees. But they are allowed to torture for five months "those people who do not have the seal of God on their foreheads" (9:4). This "seal on the forehead" recalls the people of God from 7:3-4. Like God's people in the midst of the Egyptian plagues, they are protected from harm. The scene shows, though, that the locusts carry out torture among those who do not identify with God's people.

One key message from this wild scene is that God's people have nothing to fear in the midst of God's efforts to persuade people to repent. Another key message is that the locusts are agents of Satan and carry out Satan's destructive work. The "out-of-sorts" earth is not a safe place for Jesus-believers.

Verses 7-10 describe the locusts in ways that seem to be influenced by a description in Joel 2. Evoking Joel is appropriate in that he was a prophet who interpreted a plague of locusts as God's effort to persuade people to repent. The action was successful, just as Revelation hopes this fifth trumpet scene will successfully persuade the readers to repent. One big difference between Joel and Revelation is that Revelation imagines this scene involving battle-ready locusts. The image replaces the real thing.

In John's description, the locusts variously appear as "horses equipped for battle," as humans with "faces ... like human faces ... hair like women's hair," as animals with "teeth like lions' teeth," and "tails like scorpions" (9:7-10). Their wings sound like "many chariots with horses rushing into battle" (9:9). These are imagined, not real, creatures. These locusts have a "king" or "emperor" whose name in Hebrew and Greek is "destruction" ("Apollypon," 9:11). He is at work among human beings for evil and destructive purposes contrary to God's will. Hence there is a need for people, including believers, to repent.

The blowing of the sixth trumpet releases a horrifying scene: the killing of one-third of humankind by God's agents (9:15, 18). The voice authorizing this slaughter comes "from the four horns of the golden altar before God" (9:13). The last reference to this altar in 8:2-5 identified it as the place where the prayers of God's people were being presented. Does the (imagined) slaughter come about in response to those prayers? Does it come about in response to the call for revenge of the martyrs under the altar (6:9-11)?

The voice commands the angel to "release the four angels who are bound at the great river Euphrates" (9:14). The release of the angels to "kill a third of humankind" is also a release of a colossal number of troops "of cavalry": "two hundred million" (9:16). These seem to be horses decked out for battle but they have heads "like lions' heads" (9:17). They are also agents of destruction since "fire and smoke and sulfur came out of their mouths" and killed a "third of humankind" (9:17-18).

78

Some have seen a reference in these verses to an attack from the Parthians, since the Euphrates marked the border between the Roman Empire and the Parthian Empire. Others have seen a reference to Israel's old enemies, the Assyrians and the Babylonians. Both had been God's agents in invading and punishing Israel. More likely, others see a variation on the locusts summoned by the fifth trumpet in the scene that opens chapter 9. They understand this scene to depict further agents of the devil. Again we must remember that we are reading a vision and not a historical report. The scene envisions a world under attack as a dangerous place in which to live and to be faithful to God. Chapters 12–14 will elaborate these claims.

Verses 9:20-21 reflect on the divine purposes at work through these terrible trumpet-blowing scenes. The revelation is that God is at work in the world to bring about repentance. The shocking violence and destructiveness of these scenes that envision a world falling apart and under attack call Jesus-believers in the seven cities to distance themselves from "worshiping demons and idols of gold and silver and bronze and stone and wood, which cannot see or hear or walk" (9:20). This idolatry is seen as part of a wider circle of evil comprising "murders...sorceries...fornication or...thefts" (9:21).

But the divine purposes for people to change their ways of seeing and living are not fulfilled. A change of approach and outcome follow in chapters 10–11.

# A Prophetic Task: Chapters 10–11

Mercifully, before the seventh trumpet is blown (11:15), the sequence of destruction and judgment comes to a temporary halt. There was a similar interruption or interlude after the six seals in the first sequence in chapter 7. There, the interlude of chapter 7 provided consolation and encouragement; here, chapters 10–11 provide challenge and calling.

The focus shifts from God's attempts to effect repentance through the catastrophic warnings envisioned in chapters 8–9. Chapters 10–11 show God at work in the present dangerous world through the prophetic ministry of people like John and the two witnesses of chapter 11. With this reminder comes challenge and calling for Revelation's readers to take up this same task of challenging misplaced commitments and priorities. The chapters also warn that to live against the grain is dangerous, and inevitably means suffering and rejection.

Chapter 10 is another commissioning scene. It repeats the heart of 1:9-20, where John was called or commissioned as God's instrument. Here he is recommissioned to speak God's message. This recommissioning reinforces the opening chapter's claim that John presents God's word. Its agent is an angel (10:1). Aspects of the description tell us that this angel acts on God's behalf. It comes down "from heaven"; "cloud" and "fire" indicate divine presence (see Exod 13:17-22). The rainbow recalls God's promise of mercy and faithfulness to Noah (Gen 9:8-17).

The angel holds an open "little scroll" (10:2). He shouts and "seven thunders sounded" (10:3), an image of God speaking (Ps 29:3). We would expect in an apocalyptic document like Revelation that the prophet John would hear, understand, and pass along the words of God. So John prepares to write (10:4).

Surprisingly, though, he is given a different instruction: "Seal up what the seven thunders have said, and do not write it down" (10:4). The command "seal up" means not making the message known. It is not clear what this surprising development signifies. Usually revelations are made to pass along to others, not to conceal. One possible meaning is that God has changed God's mind, replacing any further purposes of doom with a new strategy. Or possibly it signifies that God has further purposes that do not need to be revealed at this point.

The angel declares that "there will be no more delay...the mystery of God will be fulfilled" (10:6-7). The term *mystery* signifies not something strange or unknown but God's purposes that have previously been hidden but are now revealed (see Dan 2:17-30). Again, what John has in mind is not clear. Do these purposes refer to judgment and salvation being completed? Or perhaps they anticipate 11:13 whereby God's purposes for people to repent will come about.

A voice instructs John to take the scroll from the angel (10:8-9). The angel instructs John to eat the scroll, just as the prophet Ezekiel was instructed to do (Ezek 3:1-3). Eating the scroll symbolizes

80

John's embodiment of and identification with the message that he must pass on to others. The message is both sweet and sour, a word of grace and mercy as well as of challenge and suffering in difficult circumstances (10:10). John is commissioned to "prophesy again about many peoples and nations and languages and kings" (10:11). The verb *prophesy* means, as we have seen, to proclaim more than it means to predict, to forth-tell more than to foretell.

John is then told to "measure the temple of God and the altar and those who worship there" (11:1). He is told not to bother measuring "the court outside the temple" because nations will destroy it for a period of time ("forty-two months," 11:2). This action of measuring seems to represent what the rest of the chapter elaborates. The measured temple symbolizes a worshiping community, the church, and suggests a time and space protected from the destruction and harm surrounding it. This scene restates with different symbolism the sealing of God's servants in 7:3-4, repeating God's assurance of protection of them from danger, at least for a little while, in the midst of the imploding world of imperial power.

Accordingly, "two witnesses…prophesy," or preach, for the same period of time (11:3). These figures represent the prophetic witness of the church in the midst of and to a world out of sorts. John's point is that this is the role that churches in the seven cities should be carrying out. They should be questioning and challenging the priorities and commitments, practices and behaviors of their societies, rather than imitating and actively participating in idolatrous practices, for example. The two witnesses can protect themselves from harm by consuming their opponents with fire (11:5). Their witness is linked to that of Elijah ("no rain," see 1 Kgs 17:1) and Moses ("water into blood," see Exod 7:14-25), both of whom remained faithful in the midst of opposition while they spoke truth to power.

There is a limited period of time for their witness. Opposition is inevitable and it is presented as the work of the devil in resisting God's purposes for the church. So "when they have finished their testimony," they are killed by the devil, "the beast that comes up from the bottomless pit" (11:7; see the fifth trumpet, 9:1-11). Their death is greeted as good news. People disrespect their bodies by not burying them (11:9). They "gloat over them and celebrate and exchange presents" (11:10) because the witnesses challenged (and "tormented") "the inhabitants of the earth" by speaking God's truth to expose their misplaced cultural idolatries.

Their deaths are linked to the crucifixion of Jesus (11:8). Like Jesus, "the faithful witness" (1:5), and like many others through human history, including Mahatma Gandhi and Martin Luther King, Jr., they challenged unjust societal ways of living and paid the price with their lives. Yet they are vindicated by God in an act of life-giving justice. "The breath of life from God entered them, and they stood on their feet.... And they went up to heaven in a cloud" (11:11-12). The pattern is clear: faithful witness, inevitable opposition, vindication by God.

An earthquake follows. Earthquakes depict divine power and presence (Isa 29:6; Matt 27:54). This display of divine life at work gets the attention of everyone (minus the symbolic seven thousand). Using language that can describe repentance and changed commitment (Jer 13:16), they "gave glory to the God of heaven" (11:13). The divine purpose that is spelled out in 9:20-21 is imagined to be taking place here as a result not of God's judgment but of God's life-giving justice. God overcomes the opposition that the witnesses absorbed, causing many to glorify God (11:13).

Not surprisingly, the chapter ends with another scene of worship as the seventh angel blows his trumpet. The worship focuses on God's sovereign reign, or empire, that "overcomes" nations that previously did not honor God (11:15-17). Presumably, this overcoming happens because of displays of God's life-giving power, as in 11:11-13, that cause everyone to glorify God. The scene ends with a vision of God's temple—not the temples of Artemis, Zeus, or the Roman emperors—as the place where God's presence is encountered, and true and exclusive worship is to be offered.

# Study Questions

1. What observations do you have about Revelation 8–11 and this second sequence of judgment scenes?

2. These chapters are increasingly violent. What role or effect does this violence have in these visions?

3. In his attempt to change what he considers to be the overaccommodated way of living of Jesus-believers, John has adopted various tactics: warnings (chs. 2–3), an appealing vision of heavenly worship (chs. 4–5), showing how the imperial world is imploding under its own weight (chs. 6–8), and now more violent scenes intended to get people to repent (8–11). If you were giving John a job performance review in his position as God's messenger, which of his strategies would you rate as most effective? How would you assess each strategy?

# CHAPTER 8

# Revelation Reveals the Evil Powers behind the Scenes (Rev 12–14)

In addressing Jesus-believers in the seven churches in the Roman province of Asia (modern-day Turkey), the writer has made four big claims in chapters 1–11 to show why he considers some or many of them to be too accommodated to, and too immersed in, their idol-infused civic contexts. He has argued that such behavior is unacceptable because:

• cultural accommodation to the Roman imperial world is contrary to God's will (chs. 2–3);

• true worship of God the creator and redeemer permits worship of no other (chs. 4–5);

• the self-destructive and violent ways of imperial Rome enact God's judgment on the Roman Empire now in the present (chs. 6–8); and

• God is working now in the present to ensure that people repent (chs. 9–11).

Chapter 11 ended with a response of apparent repentance and many glorifying God (11:13), along with a celebration of the establishment of God's reign (11:15-19). Chapters 12–14 add a further revelation that intensifies those of chapters 6–8. This imperial world that infuses the seven cities, in which some Jesus-believers participate and which is under God's judgment, is in the control of the devil. The implication of this revelation is that Jesus-believers who are actively participating in the daily life of their cities participate in the devil's world.

Such a negative verdict on the Roman Empire is at odds with those elites in Rome and the provincial cities who saw the empire as being chosen by the gods. It clearly contrasts with Josephus's view, for example, that God had chosen and used Rome's empire. It is at odds with Jezebel's more positive evaluation. Yet it is consistent with claims made by both Matthew's Gospel and Luke's Gospel. Both Gospels see Rome's empire as being in the control of the devil (Matt 4:8-9; Luke 4:5-7).

Chapters 12–14 reveal the power at work behind the scenes. Behind the buildings, games, rituals, statues, aqueducts, festivals, taxes, commercial interactions, justice, and administrative personnel, are, according to John, evil, controlling powers that are not self-evident or visible to most Jesus-believers. The chapters reveal what many Jesus-believers have not seen, namely that the world is caught up in a cosmic struggle between good and evil, God and the devil. The accommodated believers must align themselves with God's purposes. The chapters offer images and a narrative of powers at work in and through the empire's structures. John does not think of the devil as a literal dragon (or snake).

The beasts in chapter 13 have captured popular imagination and provoked many interpreters to identify various political and religious figures as "the beast." But before we get to chapter 13 there is the very difficult chapter 12. Many have found chapter 12 and its strange imagery to be one of the most confusing chapters in all of Revelation—and that is saying something, since there is plenty of competition! The scene begins in heaven; there's a red dragon, a pregnant woman in heaven, birth pangs, a child, and a fighting archangel. The images resonate with various mythological and astrological motifs in different cultures in the ancient world. Various cultures had myths concerning combat that involved gods and beastly figures. The great altar of Zeus at Pergamum depicted such a struggle.

One such connection may well be the legend of Apollo's birth. Leto has become pregnant by Zeus. But the dragon Python, fearing a threat to his control over the Delphi oracle, tries to kill the child. He is unsuccessful, and Leto gives birth to Apollo and Artemis. This birth legend was familiar in the seven cities, and the emperor Domitian claimed a particular affinity with Apollo.

The images also resonate with various biblical stories. The woman's birth pangs have suggested to some interpreters Eve (Gen 3:16), to others the nation of Israel suffering under Babylonian imperial power and being liberated from it (Mic 4:9-10), and to others the heavenly Jerusalem or community of God's people (Rev 21:9-10). But the most important echo seems to comprise traditions about Jesus and his birth. The chapter re-presents these traditions in terms of a struggle with the devil that embraces both heaven and earth. A familiar tune is sounded in an unusual key with strange harmonies.

## The Dragon/Devil (12:1-6)

The scene begins in heaven with a "portent" or a "sign," namely "a woman clothed with the sun, with the moon under her feet, and on her head a crown of twelve stars" (12:1). She is in labor, but attention moves immediately to "a great red dragon" (12:3). His color signifies death and violence (compare the red horse in 6:3-4). His power and size are indicated by multiple heads, horns, diadems, and a destructive tail that, with a flick, dislodges "a third of the stars" (12:4). Verse 9 identifies this dragon as "the Devil and Satan, the deceiver of the whole world." Again we should remember that we are reading a vision with symbolic characters. John does not literally think of the devil as a dragon (or a snake).

Conflict between the woman and the dragon emerges in verse 4b. The dragon wants to destroy her son. This conflict recalls that between Eve and the devil narrated in Genesis 3. But that layer of symbolism gives way to another, more dominant layer. Her son is Jesus, as identified by his mission "to rule all the nations" (12:5a).

This statement of Jesus' mission is a quote from Ps 2:9. This psalm originally identified Israel's king as the agent of God's rule. As God's son and anointed one, Israel's king was to "rule all nations" (see Ps 2:9). Predictably the nations do not think this a good idea, and so they "conspire" and "plot" against God's anointed king (Ps 2:1-3). Here in verse 5, Revelation's author understands this psalm in relation to Jesus as God's anointed one, or Christ, who shares in God's rule over the nations (so 11:15). The dragon/devil is thus revealed to be in opposition to Jesus and tries to kill him.

But the devil's efforts are in vain. God protects "her child [who] was snatched away and taken to God and to his throne" (12:5). This description very briefly summarizes Jesus' ministry by referring to his crucifixion, resurrection, and ascension. Through these events, Jesus shares in the supreme power and rule of God, thereby overcoming the devil.

The rest of the chapter follows two story lines, one concerning the woman and the dragon (12:6, 13-17), and the other concerning the dragon in heaven (12:7-12). We'll follow the latter first.

# The Dragon in Heaven (12:7-12)

War breaks out in heaven (12:7) between the archangel Michael and the dragon. There is no description of the war; emphasis falls on the dragon's defeat. Defeat for the dragon means his expulsion from heaven to earth (12:9). This expulsion causes a celebration of God's rule in heaven (12:10-12a). Heaven is now completely in God's control.

But there is a warning to "the earth and the sea." Cast down to the earth, the devil's activity continues though "his time is short" (12:12). Not until the completion of God's purposes is the devil's power finally and permanently constrained (20:1-3, 7-10). In the meantime, the devil is active on earth "with great wrath" for a short time (12:12). The context of his defeat in heaven and his "short" time on earth defines the present as a difficult time for faithful Jesus-believers. But there is also some encouragement in that his wrath is short-lived.

His role on earth is as the "deceiver." The same word (translated as "beguiling") is used for Jezebel in the letter to the church in Thyatira (2:20-23). She of course teaches that eating food offered to idols and participating in civic socioeconomic occasions—including where there are images, idols, and offerings—is harmless. John's use of the common language of "deceiving" for both Jezebel and the devil allies the two with each other and with the imperial system as opponents of God's. He presents Jezebel as the devil's agent. The vision of the wrathful devil "deceiving" people on earth reveals the imperial system as being the work of the devil and in opposition to God's ways. Chapter 13 will elaborate this activity. Jesus-believers cannot, as far as Revelation's author is concerned, have any interaction with this devilish system.

## The Dragon and the Woman (12:6, 13-17)

Having survived the dragon's attack on her and her child, "the woman fled into the wilderness" (12:6). The wilderness is an ambivalent place in biblical traditions. It combines both trial and hardship, as well as freedom and protection against persecution (Exod 16). In this place in the context of the devil's wrath, the woman is sustained and protected by God for a period of time. The symbolism of the woman continues to be fluid. One moment she seems to be Israel, from whom the Messiah is born. The next moment she seems to be Mary, from whom Jesus is born. Now, with Jesus ascended into heaven, when she is both under attack but yet protected from the devil, she seems to depict the church community.

Verse 13 picks up the narrative of the devil's attack on the woman. Now that the devil has been thrown out of heaven, "he pursued the woman." God protects her with wings and a safe place (12:14). The dragon tries to drown her with a flood of evil but fails (12:15-16). Giving up on the woman, the angry dragon/devil attacks her children. Again the symbolism is fluid. These children are Jesus-believers "who keep the commandments of God and hold the testimony of Jesus" (12:17). For the author, these believers are not those who follow Jezebel but those who distance themselves from imperial society and its rituals. The scenario recognizes that opposition inevitably accompanies such non-participation. Believers are vulnerable and under attack. Yet the devil's "time is short" (12:12), so there is encouragement to them to withstand it.

# The Devil's Agents

Chapter 13 elaborates the devil's deceiving work (12:9) and attack on Jesus-believers (12:17). It reveals that this attack is carried out by means of two beasts. The first beast, described in 13:1-10, represents the Roman Empire and particularly its emperor, depicted in ways that recall the emperor Nero (54–68 C.E.), who is regarded as the epitome of evil. The second beast, described in 13:11-18, encourages people to worship the first beast and participate in imperial economic activity. This beast probably represents both imperial and provincial personnel who were based in cities, such as the seven addressed by Revelation. They organized and funded various civic occasions for imperial worship and commercial activities.

## The First Beast (13:1-10)

Out of the sea emerges a powerful beast. Verses 2 and 4 explain that the dragon or devil from chapter 12 has given its authority to this beast. "And the dragon gave it his power and his throne and great authority" (13:2). The beast represents the dragon/devil and its work against God's purposes in human society.

The beast resembles the dragon in having the same symbols of power: "ten horns...seven heads...ten diadems" (13:1). Verse 2 provides a second description in terms of powerful animals, namely leopard, bear, and lion. Verse 3 seems to parody the description of "the lamb slain but standing" (see 5:6) by describing the beast with "one of its heads [that] seemed to have received a death-blow, but its mortal wound had been healed" (13:3). This strange reference probably refers to the emperor Nero's suicide in the year 68 C.E., and rumors that developed thereafter that he had returned from the dead. The parody of the lamb "slain but standing" signals conflict between this beast and the Lamb.

The beast gains great support from "the whole earth" and from "every tribe and people and language and nation" (13:3, 7). They worship both the dragon and the beast, demonstrating that the two are allies (13:3-4, 8). John's revelation is that worship of the emperor is worship of the devil. His claim is the highly subversive one that the Roman Empire is the devil's agent. The implication is that Jesus' believers must not participate in such a world.

Verses 5-6 highlight that the beast is in opposition to God by three times referring to its "blasphemies against God." Presumably these blasphemies involve receiving worship and claiming that some dead emperors had become gods. Yet as offensive as this is, John's claim is also that the beast's present activity falls within the sovereign purposes of God and that it will not last forever even though Rome claimed to be the "eternal empire." The beast's work on behalf of the devil/dragon has an expiration date. It "was allowed to exercise authority for forty-two months" (13:5).

Further confrontation follows. Just as the Dragon attacked the woman's children (12:17), so the beast "was allowed to make war on the saints and to conquer them" (13:7). In the New Testament, the term "saints" designates followers of Jesus. It translates a word that could also be translated "holy ones," referring to those who are set apart for the service of God. There is no evidence for actual empire-wide persecution in the late first century. Rather, John envisions persecution as the inevitable consequence of people refusing to worship the beast.

Those who refuse worship are the true believers whose names are written "in the book of life" (13:8). This book was previously mentioned in 3:5 in the letter to Sardis. It draws from a Hebrew Bible image of a list or registry of those who belong to God's people (Exod 32:32-33). Faithful actions—here the refusal to join in any worship of the emperor in any form—ensure one's name is entered into this book.

The section closes with a direct appeal to Revelation's audience to understand what John is demanding (13:10). They must be willing to pay the price. There is no escape from these consequences, no "rapture," or free ticket out. Nor is there any encouragement to launch a violent attack on the empire. Instead there is only the absorption of and faithful resistance to its demands because of loyalty to Jesus. Nor does John have any patience for the tolerant participation in the imperial rituals that Jezebel advocates.

**The Second Beast (13:11-18)**

The second part of the chapter presents another beast in league with the first. This beast—also lamblike in its appearance in part— "makes the earth and its inhabitants worship the first beast"

91

(13:12). The beast's work focuses initially on the construction of imperial images, even ones that can talk. Many people have identified this beast with various political and religious figures. In John's context, those who most energetically promoted the worship of the empire were elite persons in the cities of the empire. With wealth, power, and status, they funded feasts, constructed temples and statues, led processions, and served as high priests. In doing so, they displayed and gained status and honor, showed themselves to be loyal members of the empire, formed alliances with local imperial figures like governors, and secured political, economic, and social power for themselves in cities. These are the ones John refers to as the second beast.

But we must remember that religious observation was not a separate sphere independent of political or economic matters. It was tightly intertwined with commercial and civic activities. Offerings were made, for example, to images at meetings of trade and crafts associations, and at civic gatherings in the theater. Various gods and goddesses blessed aspects of commercial and civic activity, including the food supply. If a person refused to participate in acknowledging images, he or she was isolated from commercial activity and seriously disadvantaged in terms of economic livelihood.

So the second beast "causes all, both small and great, both rich and poor, both free and slave, to be marked on the right hand or the forehead, so that no one can buy or sell who does not have the mark" (13:16-17). Like the mark that identifies true believers (7:3-4), this mark is about loyalty, ownership, and possession. Animals and slaves were marked or branded. Ezekiel was commanded to put a mark on the foreheads of those who were troubled by the "abominations" committed in Jerusalem (Ezek 9:4-6). Like that mark, this one is also an image, a picture of ownership. It is not a literal engraved mark on a person's hand or forehead. Of course the major difference between the two marks is that they identify those on either side of the cosmic struggle between God and the devil.

The second beast's mark is identified in verse 17 as "the name of the beast or the number of its name." Verse 18 identifies the mark as the number "six hundred sixty-six." In the ancient world, it was common for letters in an alphabet to have numerical values. This practice, known as gematria, is present here with the number 666.

The practice works on the assumption that people would know who was being referred to in this somewhat coded way. But it has proved difficult for subsequent readers to know for sure. The most common explanation is that the total 666 refers to the name "Nero Caesar" written in Hebrew letters. What is most significant, however, is not so much the precise identification as the type of character Nero represents. As with the wound on the beast's head (13:3), he is presented as the representative, the archetype, of the diabolical evil of the empire. He had persecuted some Jesus-believers in the city of Rome in the mid-60s for a short time. He had overseen the empire's exploitative and repressive ways. Though he had committed suicide in 68 C.E., there were rumors about his return from the dead.

# Revelation 14

Chapters 12–13 have revealed that the Roman Empire was under the devil's control. They have also revealed that practices of commerce and religious celebrations involving images were also expressions of the devil's control. Chapter 14 employs a fast-paced sequence of images—two visions and three angels—to spell out implications of this revelation.

## Vision 1 (14:1-5)

Another worship scene follows that creates important contrasts with chapter 13. Unlike the beasts, it involves the Lamb (14:1). Unlike the false worship of the dragon (13:4), beasts (13:8, 12), and images (13:14), this is "true" worship, directed toward God (14:2-3). It is offered not by those marked by the beast (13:16-17) but by those "who had his name and his Father's name written on their foreheads" (14:1). It is offered by the "one hundred forty-four thousand" who represent—the number is not literal—the whole people of God. Verse 4 describes them as those "who have not defiled themselves with women, for they are virgins." Again we have metaphorical language. One does not have to be male and celibate to participate in this worship.

The metaphor of celibacy has been understood in two main ways. Perhaps these "virgins" represent "the armies of heaven"

(19:14) who are loyal to the victorious Christ (19:11-16). This interpretation draws on the requirement of sexual abstinence before battle (so Uriah in 2 Sam 11:6-13, especially 11:11). More likely, John uses the term "virgin" because it is antithetical to the metaphor of fornication. Since chapters 2–3, borrowing the metaphor from the prophets (Hos 1–3), John has presented those who participated with Jezebel in any socioeconomic or civic activity involving idolatry as committing "fornication" (2:14, 20-21; 9:21; 18:3, 9). The opposite of unfaithfulness with the beast (fornication) is "virginity," the contrasting faithfulness to the Lamb that refuses participation in any idolatrous practice.

### A Preaching Angel (14:6-7)

The worship scene gives way to an angel "with an eternal gospel to proclaim to those who live on the earth—to every nation and tribe and language and people" (14:6). His "good news" comprises a call to "fear God...and worship" the creator of all things since judgment is coming (14:7). This angel continues the evangelizing work to turn people to God.

### A Judging Angel (14:8)

Another angel appears. This one announces judgment on Babylon, a code name for Rome, for its sin of making people participate in "fornication" or idolatry. Chapter 13 narrated the beasts' activity in promoting this worship. Chapters 15–18 will elaborate this judgment.

### Another Judging Angel (14:9-11)

A third angel appears. This angel announces judgment specifically on those who declared allegiance to the devil/beast by participating in worship activities. Verses 10-11 graphically describe their eternal punishment.

### Direct Address (14:12-13)

The author interrupts the sequence to make a direct appeal to the readers: "Here is a call for the endurance of the saints, those who keep the commandments of God and hold fast to the faith of Jesus" (14:12). This call is followed by God's promise of eternal reward for those who endure—even to death—the consequences of not participating in idolatrous worship (14:13).

### A Vision (14:14-20)

The chapter ends with a dramatic vision of "one like the Son of Man" carrying out judgment. He is the risen Christ. In 1:19 this figure, based on Dan 7:13-14, had called John to "write what you have seen," commissioning him as God's spokesperson. Now, in this awful vision, at the urging of an angel, the one like the Son of Man carries out the judgment that the second and third angel had promised. Chapters 15–18 will elaborate this judgment.

## Study Questions

1. John "reveals" that the power behind the Roman Empire is the devil (chs. 12–13). How do you understand the notion of "the devil"? Is it human wickedness writ large? A personal being opposed to God? An impersonal cosmic force? An outdated notion? Or something else?

2. Revelation 13 identifies two agents of the devil in the political structures of the empire, first the emperor and then the emperor's allies. How are these "beasts" presented? What do you think of John's approach of aligning these political powers (his enemy), with the devil?

3. One of the fundamental realities of our world is the experience of evil and suffering. Of course, this is not the only reality in our world; we also know wonder, beauty, excitement, and goodness. How do you think about and engage the evil in our world? How active should our struggle with evil be?

4. In 14:12, there is "a call for the endurance of the saints, those who keep the commandments of God and hold fast to the faith of Jesus." Do you think this verse provides a useful strategy?

CHAPTER 9

# Revelation Reveals That Time Is Up for the Eternal Empire (Rev 15–18)

Revelation continues to reveal. In urging Jesus-believers in the seven cities to distance themselves from involvement in their empire-ruled, idol-infused civic contexts, Revelation has revealed that

- cultural accommodation is contrary to God's will (chs. 2–3);

- involvement in civic and economic gatherings where idols are honored is contrary to true worship of God the creator and redeemer who allows worship of no other (chs. 4–5);

- the self-destructive and violent ways of imperial Rome enact God's judgment (chs. 6–8);

- God is also at work in the midst of the Roman empire, creating a chance for repentance (chs. 9–11); and

- the empire is in the hands of the devil (chs. 12–14).

Chapters 15–18 add another revelation. Time is up for Rome's eternal empire. There is still time for repentance, but that time is short since the completion of God's judgment of the Roman Empire is close at hand. This new revelation that time is up for the Roman Empire occurs through another set of seven judgment scenes that involve the pouring out of bowls (chs. 15–16). The seventh scene depicting Rome/Babylon's collapse is elaborated in chapters 17–18.

97

Chapters 15–16 are linked to and build on the two previous cycles of seven seals (chs. 6–8) and seven trumpets (9–11). All three cycles focus on God's judgment from three different perspectives. Chapters 6–8 show judgment taking place through the empire's own actions as it implodes and self-destructs. Chapters 9–11 show God's judgment as an opportunity for repentance. Chapters 15–16 show these judgments to be not only under way and offering a chance of repentance, but soon to be completed. God continues to work for their repentance but there is urgency. The end is near. Time is short (12:12). What then will follow? Chapters 19–22 will reveal the completion of God's purposes.

Chapters 15–16 present this imminent judgment by means of seven plagues (15:1) or the pouring out of "bowls full of the wrath of God" (15:7). As with the trumpets in chapters 8–11, this sequence of bowls again draws on the plagues in Exodus. There the plagues expressed God's purpose to have the Egyptian ruler, Pharaoh, repent, or change his heart, about freeing the people from slavery. This connection with the Exodus story underlines the chance for repentance in Rome's world as we saw in chapters 8–9. Now chapters 15–16 show that the opportunity to repent is very short.

| Revelation | Description of Plagues | Exodus |
|---|---|---|
| 16:2 | Foul and painful sores | 9:8-12 |
| 16:3 | The sea becomes blood | 7:14-25 |
| 16:4-7 | Rivers and springs become blood | 7:14-25 |
| 16:8-9 | Scorching heat from the sun | ? |
| 16:10-11 | Darkness | 10:21-23 |
| 16:12-16 | Drying up the Euphrates; spirits like frogs | 8:1-7 |
| 16:17-21 | Hail and thunder | 9:13-25 |

The repetition of three sequences of seven scenes of judgment in chapters 6–8, 8–11, and 15–16 is very striking. Why does Revelation include three sets of seven scenes of judgment? Why is it necessary to belabor the point with twenty-one scenes?

In part it seems that the need to emphasize judgment reflects the complacency and accommodation John thinks exists among some Jesus-believers. They do not recognize the compromised way in which they live. They do not see the danger of civic and socioeconomic involvement with the Roman Empire. They think idolatry and images are harmless. John tries to jolt them into a different understanding. He seeks to replace complacency with crisis. John's repeated revelation is that they participate in false worship. The empire is under judgment. It is in the control of the devil. Its end is nigh. Time is up for Rome's eternal empire. Understanding these things means Jesus-believers will repent of their participation in activities involving idols and in the empire's commercial activity.

And second, the repetition of these scenes underscores God's grace. As we have seen, John presents this lengthy sequence of scenes as a call to repentance. They are a means of disturbing the comfortable and compromised Jesus-believers in the cities in Asia. God goes to such extensive ends to secure the loyalty and faithfulness of the believers in a different way of life.

## The Seven Plagues and Bowls (Chapters 15–16)

The sequence is introduced as another vision (1:12; 5:1; 6:1; 13:11; 14:6). In heaven John sees "seven angels with seven plagues" (15:1). Twice verse 1 emphasizes the finality of the plagues. They are "the last" of the three visions of God's judgment. They signify that "the wrath of God is ended." Again we must remember that we are reading descriptions of visions, not news reports.

John also sees a worship scene involving "those who had conquered the beast and its image and the number of its name" (15:2). The reference looks back to the revelation of the beasts in chapter 13, the devilish powers "behind the throne" who promote participation in imperial and civic observances as well as commercial activity, all of which involve idolatry. Those in God's presence have "conquered the beast," which means they have not participated in idolatry. God has vindicated them.

Significantly, they worship God as all powerful ("Lord God the Almighty!") and ruler of all ("King of the nations!" 15:3). This recognition in worship of God's superiority is a political statement. It contests Rome's claims to be the supreme power that exercises rule over the world by asserting that God has all power and rules the nations. This vision of God's empire outdoes Rome's even while it imitates it! Unlike Rome's empire that comprises only conquered or allied peoples, God's reign embraces *every* nation. "All nations will come and worship before you" (15:4; see also 5:13).

Just how this situation comes about, in which all nations worship God, is not specified. However it happens, this confident celebration of all the nations worshiping God provides an important context for chapter 16. It indicates that God's purposes are focused on salvation for all peoples. And it suggests that these sequences of repentance-seeking plagues are an effective part of accomplishing this goal.

Attention moves back to the seven, plague-bearing angels who emerge from the heavenly temple. One of "the four living creatures (cf. 4:6-11) gave the seven angels seven golden bowls full of the wrath of God" (15:7). Wrath and mercy coexist, but in the end life-giving mercy seems to win the day. The chapter ends, as it began, by underscoring the plagues as the final expression of God's judgment (15:1, 8).

Chapter 16 begins with an instruction to the seven angels to "pour out on the earth the seven bowls of the wrath of God" (16:1). This instruction introduces the seven judgment scenes. The scenes, as with the trumpets in chapters 8–11, are modeled on the plagues in Exodus that were intended to change Pharaoh's mind. This rerun of the Exodus plagues underscores the plagues as a further opportunity to repent.

The first bowl, poured out on the earth, comprises "a foul and painful sore…on those who had the mark of the beast and who worshiped its image" (16:2). This mark was the work of the second beast in identifying those who expressed their loyalty to the empire by participating in civic worship and economic activity

(13:16-17). Revelation's attack on the empire, on its manifestations in idols and images, and on Jesus-believers participating in commerce and worship continues with this image of an infected sore.

The second poured-out bowl causes an ecological disaster (compare the trumpets in 8:6-12) by turning the sea into blood and killing every living sea creature (16:3). The third poured-out bowl expands the ecological disaster by turning rivers and springs into blood (16:4). This action brings declarations that God's actions are "true and just" punishment for the shedding of the blood of "saints and prophets" (16:5-7). Evoking martyred "saints and prophets" highlights the opposition to God's ways and people that defines the Roman imperial world.

The fourth poured-out bowl afflicts the sun. It causes "scorching heat" and cursing God, but not repentance (16:8-9). The reference to repentance underscores the urgency of the divine action. The fifth poured-out bowl plunges the beast's kingdom, or empire, into darkness (6:10). Again there is cursing and the failure to take advantage of the opportunity to repent (6:11). We must remember that the writing (and reading) of Revelation causes no actual damage to the earth or cosmos.

The sixth poured-out bowl involves invasion and troops assembled for battle at Armageddon (16:12-16). Initially, the scenario involves the drying up of the river Euphrates, which "[prepares] the way for the kings from the east" (16:12). Not for the first time does Revelation evoke the Parthians, Rome's rival empire to the east. One version of the legend about Nero having come back to life has him leading the Parthian armies against Rome to regain his throne.

But the scene kicks it up a notch. There is not just a threat to Rome from the east; there is also a cosmic danger and struggle. The devil/dragon and his two agents, the beast and the false prophet from chapter 13, release "three foul spirits like frogs" (16:13). "These are demonic spirits" who assemble "the kings of the whole world...for battle on the great day of God the Almighty" (16:14). The script for this vision comes from Psalm 2 where "the kings of the earth set themselves...against the LORD and his anointed" (Ps 2:1-2). The reference to "the great day" evokes a Hebrew Bible tradition in which God completes God's purposes in judgment and vindication throughout the earth (Joel 2:11, 30).

The vision is interrupted before there is a battle. The voice of the risen Jesus warns the readers that he is "coming like a thief!" (16:15). Matthew's Gospel compares Jesus the Son of Man returning to earth with a thief breaking into a house. It uses the image of a thief to warn believers to be alert and ready and not to be surprised by Jesus' sudden appearance. The warning is similar here. The Son of Man last appeared in 14:14-20 as the judge of the earth, so he has great authority. Here he offers a beatitude, or blessing, that begins "Blessed is the one..." (16:15). It uses the images of "staying awake" and "being clothed," not naked or shamed, to urge Jesus-believers to be ready for his coming. Clearly, being ready for his coming means having nothing to do with imperial and civic idolatry and images.

The last verse of the scene returns to the kings and their armies assembled for battle. It identifies the place of their assembly as being "in Hebrew...called Harmagedon" (16:16). Literally this word means "mountain of Megiddo." Popular interpretations (reading strategy 2) claim John is predicting an actual battle in north Israel. But this is not so. There is no mountain either in the text or in north Israel. Megiddo is actually situated on a plain near Mount Carmel. Nor does John describe or predict a battle. There is no need for a final battle between God and the forces of evil because God has already won that struggle in the crucifixion and resurrection of Jesus, the Lamb slain but standing and now vindicated with God in the heavens (5:6). In this act God overcomes Roman power expressed in the crucifixion of Jesus and justly restores Jesus to life. Megiddo is evoked because King Josiah of Judah had been defeated and killed there (2 Kgs 23:29-30). It is a symbol of defeat and disaster.

The seventh bowl is poured out "into the air" and God declares from the heavenly temple and throne the completion of the plagues or displays of God's wrath (16:17). This wrath is depicted as being directed against Rome and its supporters in provincial cities like the seven cities of Asia that have not repented of their exploitative and unjust imperial ways. The consequences are devastating. Accompanied by "flashes of lightning, rumblings, peals of thunder," an off-the-scale "violent earthquake" splits "the great city" Babylon into three, destroys other cities, decimates islands and mountains, and rains huge hailstones (16:18-21, especially vv.

102

18-19). The city Babylon—code-talk for Rome—"made all nations drink of the wine of the wrath of her fornication" (14:8); now the city drinks "the wine-cup of the fury of [God's] wrath" (16:19). Though intended to bring about repentance, this last plague has the opposite effect in causing some to curse God (16:21). Remember, Revelation presents—in dramatic and graphic ways— the claim that God's purposes are not to be ignored.

## Rome's Destruction: Revelation 17–18

Revelation does not hurry over this fantasy of the violent destruction of Rome. Having referred to it in 14:8 and 16:19, chapters 17–18 pause to elaborate this fantasy of Rome's certain downfall. Chapter 17 offers some graphic presentation. Chapter 18 declares that the demise of Rome, "a dwelling place of demons" (18:2), is God's will from heaven (18:1-8). Then three groups who were key participants in the empire's commercial and economic life lament its destruction (18:9-20) followed by a loud angelic proclamation of judgment (18:21-26).

This prolonged celebration of Rome's envisioned fall resembles other biblical passages that glory in the demise of powerful cities. In Isaiah 23, the prophet rejoices over the fall of the important cities of Tyre and Sidon, perhaps at the hands of the Assyrians in 701 B.C.E. The passage particularly celebrates the loss of Tyre's commercial and trading power (Isa 23:1, 3, 8). It also identifies Tyre as a prostitute, as Revelation does in chapter 18, and it uses the same metaphor to depict her interaction with the nations (Isa 23:16-17). In a somewhat similar passage, another prophet, Ezekiel, also celebrates the demise of the city Tyre (Ezek 27–28). Its offenses include exalting itself (Ezek 28:2, 9, "I am a god") and procuring abundant wealth that enrich the few and powerful (Ezek 27:33; 28:16-18). Jeremiah similarly celebrates the demise of the great city Babylon, who had extended power over large amounts of territory, including Judea (Jer 51:24-58): "the time is surely coming, says the LORD, when I will punish her idols" (Jer 51:52).

Revelation 17–18 presents Rome as a defeated woman. This presentation may well be influenced by Rome's protective warrior-goddess Roma. The identification of the woman as Rome is made

103

quite explicit in 17:18: "The woman you saw is the great city that rules over the kings of the earth." This identification is anticipated with a geographical reference to Rome's seven mountains (17:9) and with references to the line of emperors (17:9-12).

In describing the defeated and condemned woman, chapter 17 highlights various aspects of Rome's extensive power and rule, now defeated.

- The description in verse 1 of her control over "many waters" refers to Rome's political, social, and military reach. Verse 15 describes the waters as the "peoples and multitudes and nations and languages" that compose Rome's empire.

- Verse 2 references her alliances with "the kings of the earth," one of the chief ways that Rome exercised its power.

- Verse 3 presents her as riding "a scarlet beast that was full of blasphemous names," which recalls the beasts of chapter 13. The first beast (the empire) had "blasphemous names" on its head, signifying its opposition to God (13:1). The linking of the woman Rome with the beast, the agent of the devil, presents Rome as the agent of the devil. Verse 17 notes that Rome exercises its authority for a short time.

- Verse 4 presents her in imperial colors ("clothed in purple and scarlet") and with great wealth, "adorned with gold and jewels and pearls."

- Verse 4 also presents her in God's perspective as deserving judgment for her promotion of idolatry—"full of abominations and the impurities of her fornication."

- Verse 5 identifies her as "Babylon the great, mother of whores [prostitutes] and of earth's abominations." Babylon is a consistent code name in Revelation for the Roman Empire. As with Jezebel in Rev 2:20-21, John again presents his enemy as a sexually disreputable woman.

- Verse 6 probably recalls Nero's short but deadly attack on Jesus-believers in the 60s C.E. Their murder perhaps represents all those killed by the Roman quest for power, wealth, and dominance. Rome's double sins are idolatry (17:4) and murder (17:6).

- Verse 8 includes some further elaboration from an angel who emphasizes the certain destruction of the beast.

- Verses 13-14 present those who submit to the beast (agent of the devil) as being opposed to the Lamb, the "Lord of lords and King of kings," who overcomes them.

- But significantly, some of those whom the woman/city rule rebel against her and destroy her (17:15-18).

One of the disturbing features of this presentation of condemned Rome as a woman is the repeated use of the metaphors of "whore/prostitute" and "fornication." Rome is introduced in verse 1 as "the great whore," in verse 5 as the "mother of whores," and in verses 15-16 as the whore who will be made "desolate and naked" and consumed by fire. Those who ally themselves with her are said to commit fornication with her (17:2, 4; 18:3, 9). Both words, *whore* and *fornication*, share the same origin in Greek. The metaphor appeared in the letters of chapter 2 (vv. 14, 20-21) to condemn participation by Jesus-believers in Gentile culture (cf. Ps 106:34-39), notably eating food offered to idols and honoring images.

In the opening section of chapter 18 (vv. 1-9), a heavenly angel declares that Babylon/Rome has fallen. The angel declares it has been a "dwelling place of demons" (18:2) to underline its alliance with the devil and the beasts from chapter 13. While idols and economic activity have been to the fore previously, chapter 18 highlights economics and trade: "the kings of the earth have committed fornication with her, / and the merchants of the earth have grown rich from the power of her luxury" (18:3). John's call, by way of a heavenly voice, is for Jesus-believers to distance themselves from such participation: "Come out of her, my people, so that you do not take part in her sins, and so that you do not share in her plagues" (18:4).

After this heavenly announcement, three groups who were key participants in the empire's political, commercial, and economic life lament its destruction (18:9-20). First, allied client kings, "the kings of the earth, who committed fornication and lived in luxury with her," weep for "the mighty city" (18:9-10). Second, "merchants of the earth" mourn for the city and for the fact that "no one buys their cargo" (18:11). Their lament emphasizes Rome's great wealth (18:14, 16, 17a). Verses 12-13 provide a stunning list of nearly thirty resources and largely luxury items that were shipped from the provinces of the empire to Rome. The list ends with "slaves—and human lives," a tragic reminder of the human cost of the empire's economy based on slavery. Empires always control and appropriate resources for the benefit of the ruling elite and at the expense of the rest (18:11-17a). Third, "all shipmasters and sea-farers, sailors and all whose trade is on the sea" lament the fall of the "great city," recognizing that "all who had ships at sea / grew rich by her wealth!" (18:19).

The chapter ends with a further celebration of Rome's fall. Verse 20 calls the "saints and apostles and prophets" in heaven—those who in 6:9-11 cried out for God to act—to rejoice because "God has given judgment for you against her" (18:20; compare 16:4-7). Verse 21 reenacts the judgment of Rome being "thrown down" and goes on to catalog what is destroyed with the city. Music and entertainment disappear, as do artisans and trades (18:22), house-holds, and commerce (18:23). Revelation charges that Rome has "deceived" the nations with idolatry and exploitative economic practices, but supremely it has done violence to human beings. It has destroyed not only "prophets" who have announced God's purposes but also "all who have been slaughtered on earth" (18:24).

Chapters 15–18 offer this stunning vision of Rome's destruction and judgment. In the late first century, Rome's empire was power-ful, extensive, and very much in control, yet John boldly and audaciously declares its demise. The result is the proclamation that Rome, the "eternal empire," like all empires, is not eternal in God's purposes. The clear implication is that it would be a mis-take for Jesus-believers through civic, commercial, and idolatrous practices to align their own destinies with this, or any, empire, except (ironically) "the kingdom [or empire] of our Lord" (11:15) who is "Lord God the Almighty.../ King of the nations" (15:3; see also 16:7).

# Study Questions

1. In chapters 15–16, a third sequence of judgments portrayed as plagues leads up to the final destruction of Rome. These plagues (following the seven seals in chs. 6–8 and the seven trumpets in chs. 9–11) echo the plagues sent on Pharaoh in Exodus 7–11. What is the significance of echoing the Exodus story?

2. A couple of hundred years ahead of his time, John boldly declares the destruction of Rome's empire. Do you see God working God's purposes out in human history in this way, bringing down empires and raising up rulers? If not, what is God's role in human history, if any?

3. Why is Rome condemned in chapter 18? What are its failings? What effect does the chapter have on you?

4. John calls God's people to "come out from her" (18:4). What does this strategy of retreat, or withdrawal, look like in our everyday life?

# CHAPTER 10

# Revelation Reveals the Coming Triumph of God (Rev 19–22)

Revelation ends with yet another audacious revelation. It has already envisioned that, despite all appearances to the contrary, the so-called "eternal empire" of Rome is ending (chs. 15–18). In God's perspective, this empire is under God's judgment (chs. 6–18) and under the power of the devil (chs. 12–14). It has not taken the opportunity to repent (9:20; 16:9-11), so its destruction is inevitable (chs. 17–18). These are stunning claims for folks in the late first century, when Rome's empire seemed very permanent and very much in control.

Chapters 19–22 follow up this stunning announcement with another one. They tell the rest of the story. They reveal that the fulfillment of the world's destiny lies in God's hands, not with Rome. God will complete God's good and gracious purposes for human history.

This final revelation is so bold. Everything in the seven cities addressed by Revelation seems to declare the exact opposite. Roman power seems permanent. Its ways of structuring the world to benefit the powerful and wealthy elites at the expense of the rest seem to stay forever. It does not seem to be in any danger. The judgment, demonic allegiance, and demise that Revelation has proclaimed in chapters 6–18 seem nowhere in sight. The communities of Jesus-believers are small and divided. Yet chapters 19–22 reveal that the future has no place for Rome's empire. God's future comprises the establishment of God's good order.

So what does this post-empire world look like? Chapters 19–22 open with another worship scene (19:1-10), in which the "great multitude in heaven" praises God for the destruction of the Roman empire (19:1). They declare that God's "judgments are true and just; / he has judged the great whore / who corrupted the earth with her fornication, / and he has avenged on her the blood of his servants" (19:2). They go on to rejoice that "the Lord our God / the Almighty reigns" (19:6). The post–Roman Empire world comprises God's reign, or empire.

What does God's reign look like? Chapters 19–22 bring to a conclusion this theme that has been central to the whole book of Revelation. It sets out seven scenes that represent aspects of God's final reign.

After the worship scene (19:1-10), seven scenes follow:

- 19:11-16: the rider on the white horse

- 19:17-21: the defeat of the beasts and their supporters

- 20:1-3: the locking up of the devil

- 20:4-6: Christ and the saints rule

- 20:7-10: the defeat of the devil

- 20:11-15: the last judgment

- 21:1–22:5: a new heaven, new earth, and new Jerusalem

Attention to several questions is important for how we interpret these scenes. Are these scenes oriented only to the future, or does the writer of Revelation see these realities as being already under way even in the present, albeit incompletely? Are these seven scenes a sequence or timetable of "last," or final, eschatological events that begin with the rider on the white horse and culminate with the new heaven and earth? Or do the seven scenes present seven variations on the same theme? Are they seven simultaneous and overlapping visions imagining the full and final establishment of God's purposes?

These questions are best answered by recalling the claims of verse 6 that "the Lord our God / the Almighty reigns." The verb

110

*reigns* is a present-tense verb, not a future-tense one. This choice of tense suggests that these scenes depict something that is already under way. This is supported, for example, by the limits put on Death and Hades in 6:8, where "they were given authority over a fourth of the earth." Even now God asserts God's reign by restricting their influence. Likewise in chapter 12, the devil is thrown out of heaven to earth (12:9-12). Heaven becomes a devil-free zone where God's reign is now established in full: "Now have come the salvation and the power / and the kingdom of our God / and the authority of his Messiah" (12:10a). The devil's activity is limited to "the earth and the sea" and "his time is short" (12:12). These scenes, along with others, suggest that the reality of God's reign depicted in chapters 19–22 is already under way but not yet established in full. There are both present and future dimensions to these scenes.

Do they present a schedule, or timetable, of individual future events whereby God's reign is established? Or do they present different aspects of and simultaneous perspectives on the establishment of God's reign? The latter is a more convincing approach. It is difficult to make a coherent schedule and convincing sequence out of the scenes. The devil is confined twice, once for the one-thousand-year reign (20:3), but then again after a time of further rebellion (20:7-10). Judgment does not occur only in 20:11-15 but also in the second (19:17-21), fourth (20:4-6), and fifth scenes (20:7-10). The "kings of the earth" are condemned (19:17-21), yet in the last scene they are welcomed as they "bring their glory into" the New Jerusalem (21:24).The scenes portray different dimensions of God's reign.

The scenes then do not offer a chronological schedule, or timetable, of successive final events. Rather, it is better to think of them as a series of overlapping visions. They find their center in the theme of the final and full establishment of God's purposes. They develop different aspects of this theme. They offer a series of multilayered visions of God's coming victory and triumph. They engage our imagination with constantly changing visions. Across the ages, artists have frequently expressed these scenes in pictorial form. We can think of them as a series of paintings in which artists are exhibiting on the theme of the coming triumph of "the Lord our God the Almighty."

# Painting 1: The Rider on the White Horse (19:11-16)

Unlike the white horse of earthly imperial conquest and judgment (6:1-2), this is a heavenly white horse. It is ridden by the exalted Christ, identified as "Faithful and True," the judge (19:11), "The Word of God" (19:13), and "'King of kings and Lord of Lords'" (19:16). Ironically, he is presented in military terms (19:11), with "armies of heaven . . . on white horses" (19:14), yet his means of victory is not military conquest. Rather, he gains victory by his own death ("robe dipped in blood," 19:13; compare 5:1-7), and the proclamation of his prophetic and proclaiming words ("from his mouth comes a sharp sword"; 19:15; cf. Isa 49:2). He is exalted after overcoming Roman power through his crucifixion and resurrection, which reveal the limits of Roman power. His task in heaven is "to strike down the nations," "rule them," and express "the fury of the wrath of God the Almighty" (19:15). The vision pictures the exalted Christ as sharing and manifesting God's rule over all nations, including Rome. Ironically, at the same time that the scene expresses opposition to and victory over Rome's empire, it imitates aspects of it in employing military imagery and overcoming opposition.

# Painting 2: The Defeat of the Beasts and Their Supporters (19:17-21)

The heart of this scene involves the capture and destruction of the devil's agents, the two beasts, in the lake of fire. These beasts figured in chapter 13 as agents of the devil, one being the Roman Empire, and the other the allied elites, imperial officials, and those loyal to them in provincial cities, who promoted worship of images and participation in economic activity (19:20). The painting has elements of a battle scene with "the kings of the earth" gathering their armies to fight against the exalted Christ and his army (19:19). This scene recalls the gathering at Harmagedon in 16:16. Birds are summoned to eat "the flesh of kings . . . captains . . . the mighty . . . horses and their riders" as well as the "flesh of all, both free and slave, both small and great" (19:18).

The surreal nature of the scene, though, is underlined by the fact that the previous painting has shown the exalted Christ to be in heaven, not on earth. And the beasts' supporters are killed by the "sword that came from [the] mouth" of the exalted Christ, that is, by his words (19:21). He does not have an actual sword. There is no actual battle on earth. No armies fight. The beasts are captured without any warfare. The explicit references in 19:20 to the second beast's role in "[deceiving] those who had received the mark of the beast and those who worshiped its image" recalls 13:11-18. The destiny of the two beasts is "the lake of fire that burns with sulfur" (19:20; compare 14:9-11).

## Painting 3: The Locking up of the Devil (20:1-3)

With the devil's agents confined, this scene presents the locking up of "the dragon, that ancient serpent, who is the Devil and Satan" (20:2). The devilish power behind the empire revealed in chapters 12–14 is condemned. An angel from heaven accomplishes this task, the devil is thrown into a "locked and sealed" pit, or abyss, the dwelling place of demons, for a "thousand years" (20:3; see also 9:2). The number is not literal but symbolically represents a very long time. The devil's demise means he will not "deceive the nations" anymore (20:3).

## Painting 4: Christ and the Saints Rule (20:4-6)

The fourth painting shifts attention away from the demise of God's adversaries to the vindication, or resurrection, of those who have remained loyal to the exalted Christ. This vindication is presented in a throne room scene in which the resurrected ones share in the reign and power of God (compare chs. 4–5) as priests of God and of Christ (20:6). This rule lasts for a thousand years, the same symbolic number as that of the locking up of Satan (20:2). Those vindicated "had not worshiped the beast or its image and had not received its mark on their foreheads or their hands" (20:4). Again the beasts' work in chapter 13 as the agents of the devil in promoting imperial practice and power is to the fore. And again Revelation emphasizes that there can be

113

no involvement in idol worship by Jesus-believers if they are to be vindicated.

Their vindication comprises resurrection. The understanding of resurrection emerged clearly in the second century B.C.E. in the context of the struggle against the Syrian or Seleucid tyrant Antiochus IV Epiphanes. Antiochus banned worship of God and observance of the Torah practices such as circumcision, food purity, and Sabbath. Some Judeans complied; others defied the bans and paid for it with their lives. What reward is there for such faithfulness? The notion of resurrection affirmed that God's faithfulness and power extend beyond death. Their faithful deaths were not in vain. God's resurrecting power restores the faithful to life in the presence and purposes of God (see 1 Macc 1; 2 Macc 6–7; Dan 12).

This scene, then, affirms the life-giving justice of God that extends beyond death. With such certain and powerful faithfulness in view, Revelation again encourages Jesus-believers to distance themselves from their image- and idol-pervaded society.

## Painting 5: The Defeat of the Devil (20:7-10)

Another scene depicts the destruction of the devil and his allies. Typically, the devil, also called Satan here, "[deceives] the nations...Gog and Magog" and prepares them for battle (20:7). Gog is mentioned in Ezekiel 38–39. There he is identified as "Gog, of the land of Magog," (Ezek 38:1), a symbolic figure who represents militaristic and imperial powers arrayed against God and God's people. Gog and his armies are defeated. Revelation 20 presents Magog as a figure, not a land, but continues with the presentation of these figures as enemies of God and so allied with the devil.

In verse 9, they assemble for battle surrounding "the beloved city." This is the fourth reference to a "final battle" (see 16:12-16; 17:14; 19:11-21; 20:7-10), but again there is no fighting. God destroys the armies of Gog and Magog with fire (20:9). Again "the devil who had deceived them was thrown into the lake of fire and sulfur, where the beast and the false prophet were, and they will be tormented day and night forever and ever" (20:10; compare 19:19-21; 20:1-3).

114

## Painting 6: The Last Judgment (20:11-15)

This picture returns to God's throne room (4:2), but it is not a worship scene. Rather, the scene presents the Final Judgment. First, "earth and the heaven fled from his presence" (20:11) and will be replaced by a new heaven and earth (21:1). All of creation will be renewed. The scene is peopled by "the dead, great and small, standing before the throne" (20:12). They come from the sea and from Death and Hades, the dwelling place of the dead (20:13). Books are opened (Dan 7:10) and "the dead were judged according to their works, as recorded in the books" (20:12). This focus places the emphasis on how people have lived. They have not honored idols and images nor participated in compromised economic activity (20:4). For those who have not lived accordingly, their fate is "the lake of fire," not an eternal torture chamber but a place of destruction (20:15).

Yet there is another reality at work, another book, "the book of life" (20:12, 15) that God keeps "from the foundation of the world" (13:8; 17:8). This is the book of salvation constituted by God's grace that seems at least in 5:13 and 15:4 (and 21:24) to bring "all nations" to worship before God. The two books exist in tension, holding together grace and works, God's faithful commitment that all the families of the world be blessed (Gen 12:1-3), and the need for faithful human response.

After the judgment of humans comes the death of death. "Death and Hades were thrown into the lake of fire" (20:14). This is the same destiny as that of the beast and false prophet (19:20) as well as of the devil (20:10). These powers, manifested in Rome's empire and resistant to God's purposes, are systematically destroyed and have no place in the new world created by God's life-giving purposes.

## Painting 7: A New Heaven, New Earth, and New Jerusalem (21:1–22:5)

This seventh picture is the most detailed of the seven. It begins with a new heaven and new earth (21:1). A city comes down to earth from God (the New Jerusalem, 21:2). Strangely, while reading strategy 2—that we discussed in chapter 1—sees Jesus-believers being "raptured" up into heaven, Revelation actually pictures the exact opposite happening. The city comes down from God to earth.

This new city indicates the communal and relational nature of God's purposes. It stands in contrast to the seven cities in the province of Asia that defy God's purposes with idolatry and economic greed as part of Rome's empire. The city is also compared to a bride, a common image in the Prophets for both faithful and unfaithful relationship (Hos 2:19; Isa 54:6).

The essential feature of this descending city is that God dwells among humans. Verse 3 uses the plural term "peoples" to suggest the all-encompassing nature of God's presence among humans and the community this presence creates (21:3). God renews the world so that it is marked only by God's good purposes. This renewed world has no place for tears, death, mourning, crying, and pain (21:4-5). The essence of God's presence is experienced in life (21:6). There is a river and a tree of life (22:1-2). God's presence is also experienced in faithful covenant relationship ("I will be their God and they will be my children," 21:7). There is no place for sin (21:8).

The rest of the scene describes the city. Since it comes down from God, it predictably reflects the glory and radiance of God (21:11). "It has a great, high wall" but it also has "twelve gates…inscribed [with] the names of the twelve tribes of the Israelites," signaling continuity with Israel (21:12). The wall also has "twelve foundations, and on them are the twelve names of the twelve apostles of the Lamb" (21:14). The gates are always open, allowing "the nations…and the kings of the earth" to enter into the city (21:24). The scene in 19:17-21 pictured the kings' destruction, but this scene images their inclusion in God's good purposes. To be able to include all people, the city's measurements indicate a massive, cube-shaped city of "fifteen hundred miles; its length and width and height are equal" (21:16). It is built from precious stones and metals (21:18-21).

Not surprisingly, it does not include a temple, "for its temple is the Lord God the Almighty and the Lamb" (21:22). Worship is continual (22:3). Not only does this lack of a temple underline the city's key feature of God's pervasive presence, it also contrasts this city with the seven cities in Asia, where temples and idols were a dominant and troubling feature. Its inhabitants are the nations and kings of the earth. Previously, they seem to have been condemned (19:15; 20:7-9), but now, consistent with 5:13, 15:4, and 21:24, they are redeemed in right relationship with God. They walk in the light, the presence and salvation of God who guides them (21:24; 22:5). They bring their honor or splendor to God (21:26). This is the "healing of the nations" (22:2), which, it seems, God has brought about through the seals, the plagues of the trumpets, and the bowls of wrath (chs. 6–18). They bear God's name "on their foreheads," signifying their allegiance (22:4; 7:3 [contrast the beast's mark, 13:16]). God's patient restraint, God's powerful mercy, has won the day.

## Conclusion (22:6-21)

The document ends with a series of appeals, warnings, and blessings for the reader. Some of the material resembles the statements of chapter 1, which present John as God's commissioned and authoritative prophet or spokesperson (22:8-9). Some exhorts the readers to put the teaching into practice. So verse 6 underlines that "these words are trustworthy and true" because they originate with "the Lord, the God" and "his angel" (22:6). The imminence of Jesus' return emphasizes urgency for readers to keep these words and worship God (22:7-9, 12). Accordingly, the angel also commands John not to seal up the prophecy but to make it available because "the time is near" (22:10). The words will be divisive—the evil will ignore them and the righteous will obey them (22:11).

Further authority is added with the risen Jesus declaring his imminent return and identifying himself as "the Alpha and the Omega, the first and the last, the beginning and the end" (22:13). He offers a blessing on those who remain faithful in contrast to those "outside...who [love] and [practice] falsehood" (22:15). And he testifies that he is the origin of the message (22:16). The Spirit and the bride (the faithful church) welcome his return (22:17).

Then follows a warning against adding any teaching to this

book on pain of experiencing the plagues described in chapters 8–16 (22:18). Likewise, removing any content means losing one's share in God's purposes (22:19). The book ends with another cry for Jesus to return to complete God's purposes (22:20) and a final benediction, "The grace of the Lord Jesus be with all the saints. Amen" (22:21).

## Study Questions

1. Look back over the seven overlapping scenes or "paintings" of the establishment of God's good and just purposes in 19:11–22:5. Which ones do you find especially appealing and why?

2. If you were to create an eighth picture of the establishment of God's good and just purposes, describe what it would look like. Or, even better, draw it!

3. Chapter 22 ends as the book of Revelation begins—with an underscoring of John's authority that we as readers are supposed to recognize. But clearly some in the churches, such as Jezebel, did not recognize his authority or appreciate his style of presentation. Nor did they appreciate his demand that they "come out from" their everyday culture. Having worked through Revelation now, how has your thinking about this book changed or stayed the same? For example, have you come to a fresh appreciation of some aspects of the book? Which ones? Do you have a strong dislike for parts of it? If you had to choose between John's or Jezebel's point of view on cultural involvement, which one would you choose and why?

CHAPTER 11

# Should Revelation Be Left Behind? Reading Revelation Today

We have framed our discussion of Revelation around the question, What does Revelation reveal? We have set about answering this question by identifying eight dimensions of Revelation's revelation:

- It is God's word for God's world (ch. 1);

- Cultural accommodation is dangerous (chs. 2–3)

- True worship centers on God the creator and Jesus the redeemer (chs. 4–5)

- Judgment is taking place now (chs. 6–7)

- God is at work giving the world a chance to repent (chs. 8–11)

- The Roman Empire is in the hands of the devil (chs. 12–14)

- Time is up for Rome's eternal empire (chs. 15–18)

- The triumph of God is coming (chs. 19–22)

These affirmations raise some important theological and pastoral issues. In this last chapter, we will take up just five issues and think about their implications for contemporary readers of Revelation.

# 1. Empires and God's Purposes

Revelation's verdict on Rome's empire is clear. Without acknowledging that empires with vast resources of people and resources can do much good, John delivers a consistently negative and harsh verdict on the Roman Empire. Followers of Jesus should not be actively involved in it (chs. 2–3). It is under God's judgment in the present (6–8). It is under the devil's control (chs. 12–14). Its future demise is certain (chs. 15–18). It will be replaced by God's empire (19–22). John especially attacks those who follow the teaching of Jezebel and who think involvement in imperial society is harmless.

Does this perspective have anything to say to contemporary readers of Revelation? In the past, readers have understood Revelation to condemn tyrants like Hitler and the racist structures of apartheid in South Africa. What about contemporary readers of Revelation in the United States, who live at the heart of, arguably, the most powerful military, economic, and cultural empire the world has ever known? Does Revelation have anything to say to us who are culturally deeply embedded in our society, who like to think of our country as a shining light for the rest of the world, and who like to think that we use our massive power for the good of other countries?

Now as then, it is hard for those who are in the midst of an empire to remain unaffected by how empires think and act. For instance, empires frequently assert that they have a right to interfere in the affairs of other countries. Empires commonly create two groups of people, "the haves," who benefit, and the "have nots," whose lives are not improved in any way. The haves typically benefit from the economy's well-being and enjoy cultural practices like entertainment, prosperity, comfort, and whatever they need, with little consideration for the have nots. Empires rarely consider the cost to other countries and people of maintaining their lifestyle, and they never consider giving any of that up. And empires are quite happy to claim God's blessing for all of this. It is this way of thinking and acting that John confronts as being opposed to God's way of acting in the lamb that was slain but is now standing.

Hence John creates this dualistic way of thinking, contrasting

120

Jezebel's accommodation with the empire with his own fierce opposition. Of course, one of the risks of communicating with an either-or scheme is that it is does not adequately match the complexities of living in the empire. Another risk of communicating with such passionate and harsh analysis is that it can be very alienating. People who have been immersed in and are the beneficiaries of empire can consume its propaganda and may not recognize the dangers John is naming. But one of the strengths of communicating with vivid and repeated scenes is that John's points can seep through defenses. One of the consequences of Revelation being in the church's Scriptures is that John won't just go away and be quiet, no matter how uncomfortable he might make the beneficiaries of empire feel.

Whatever we think of his answers, he does ask hard questions of our discipleship.

- He asks whether we have settled for mammon rather than God.

- He wonders who or what we worship.

- He asks us how we think about the societal "good," about matters of justice and the right of all people to adequate resources for life, and about how that thinking might shape our living.

- He asks us about our fascination with power, with "might is right," with self-interest, and whether those values and structures are best for our life together on planet Earth.

- He wonders about the size of our hearts, whether we comprehend the passion of God for the well-being of all people, and whether that makes any difference to our living.

- He wonders if we have understood God to be working in the world for the benefit of all people, not just a privileged few, and whether we have aligned our lives with God's purposes in personal, communal, and national matters.

- He asks about our ultimate loyalties, whether anyone or anything usurps God's central place in our lives, under what circumstances, and with what impact.

121

## 2. What Is God Doing in the World?

Revelation is very much about God and God's purposes for the world. So how does Revelation envision God's purposes and presence at work in people's lives? How do we name God's purposes and our experiences of God's presence (or absence) in our world and in our own lives? What, if anything, is God doing in the world?

Perhaps the dominant impression from Revelation is that of God judging the world. This is not surprising given that a significant part of Revelation's content centers on the three cycles of seven scenes of judgment in chapters 6–18. The seven seals (chs. 6–7) are followed by seven trumpets (chs. 8–11) and then the seven bowls of wrath (chs. 15–16), the seventh concerning Rome's destruction being elaborated in chapters 17–18. To many people Revelation seems to be a profoundly pessimistic book in which God condemns the world.

But as we have seen, it is not this simple. In discussing the seven seals, for example, we noticed that God is not aggressively and proactively hurling thunderbolts at the world in order to destroy it. Rather, God allows the world to experience the destructive consequences of its own imperial ways and structures. Why does God do this? The use of the Exodus plagues as the basis for the scenes involving the seven trumpets and bowls (chs. 8–11, 15–16) indicates that God's purposes involve saving rather than condemning the world. The plagues were intended to give Pharaoh a chance to change his mind and let the people go free. Likewise, Revelation presents the trumpets and the bowls as giving the world a chance to repent (9:20-21; 16:9, 11). God works to rescue or save the world from itself.

But is God effective in accomplishing these purposes? It seems in chapters 9 and 16 that God's purposes come to naught. The world does not repent. It is under the power of the devil, manifested in imperial structures and by provincial elites who encourage active involvement in recognizing Rome's divine sanctions and economic activity (chs. 12–13). This seemingly pessimistic view of humans defying God seems to be confirmed in the vision of Rome's demise in chapters 17–18. God appears to be unable to accomplish God's saving purposes.

Yet this also is not the whole story. The regularly recurring worship scenes celebrate God as establishing God's purposes.

"Salvation belongs to our God who is seated on the throne, and to the Lamb!" (7:10)

"The kingdom of the world has become the kingdom of our Lord / and of his Messiah, / and he will reign forever and ever." (11:15)

In chapter 11, after the two witnesses have been killed but vindicated by God, "the rest [of the people]...gave glory to the God of heaven" (11:13).

The expulsion of the dragon/devil from heaven in chapter 12 establishes heaven as a Satan-free zone where God's reign is now established: "Now have come the salvation and the power / and the kingdom of our God / and the authority of his Messiah, / for the accuser of our comrades has been thrown down" (12:10).

The establishment of heaven as the realm of God's rule anticipates its establishment on earth since the devil's impact on earth is temporary: "his time is short" (12:12). In addition, Revelation envisions all creation caught up in the experience of God's salvation:

Then I heard every creature in heaven and on earth and under the earth and in the sea, and all that is in them, singing, "To the one seated on the throne." (5:13)

Revelation declares confidently, "All nations will come / and worship before you, / for your judgments have been revealed" (15:4). And in envisioning the final establishment of God's purposes, it presents the light of the New Jerusalem as drawing all the nations into it to worship God, even former enemies such as "the kings of the earth":

for the glory of God is its light, and its lamp is the Lamb. The nations will walk by its light, and the kings of the earth will bring their glory into it. Its gates will never be shut by day....People will bring into it the glory and the honor of the nations. (Rev 21:23-26)

The ultimate establishment of God's purposes means the healing of the nations (22:3). Revelation ends with this declaration of

123

the successful accomplishment of God's purposes that restores all creation. It is a profoundly optimistic and hopeful book.

Revelation thus sets up a paradox that holds together God's justice and God's mercy for all. On one hand it declares that God's ways are "just and true" (15:3) in ending the idolatrous and exploitative ways of the Roman Empire (see also 16:7; 19:2). On the other hand, it celebrates God's all-inclusive, life-giving, and salvific purposes that ultimately reconcile and heal the nations (22:3), finding a place for them and their kings and all people and nations in God's new heaven and earth (5:13; 15:4; 21:23-26). Revelation does not attempt to reconcile this paradox. It affirms both dimensions. But by placing the visions of God's triumph over all at the end of the book in chapters 19–22, it ends optimistically and hopefully with a proclamation that God's inclusive mercy wins out.

Yet there is an irony about this paradoxical presentation of God's purposes. As much as Revelation resists imperial ways, it imitates them in its vision of God's purposes. The vision of God conquering all reinscribes imperial ways. It presents God doing the same sort of thing that the Roman Empire does.

# 3. Violence

To think about God's ways of justice and mercy raises the question of the role of violence in Revelation. From the beginning to the end, the book constantly envisions violence. The Son of God threatens to throw Jezebel onto a bed and kill her children (2:21-23). Chapter 8 presents a vision of terrible violence against creation with a third of the earth, trees, sea, rivers, sun, moon, and stars destroyed (8:7-12), alongside a third of human beings (9:18). In chapter 19 the birds are invited to come and feast on the flesh of kings, military personnel, free and slave who gather to wage war against the exalted, heavenly Christ (19:17-21). God seems to be hateful and full of vengeance. These sustained fantasies of violence are very disturbing. How do we understand them?

Throughout the book, I have emphasized that no actual people, rivers, oceans, trees, or planets were harmed in the production of Revelation. The book employs visions, not news reports. It imagines, not prescribes. It uses the visions to present theological insights. It imagines these terrible disasters as a means of graphically presenting theological truths. It does not prescribe or predict such disasters.

So in 6:1-4 it envisions four horsemen who depict the normal activities of empire, namely conquest, war, economic exploitation, famine, pestilence, and death. These visions picture God's permissive stance toward the Roman Empire in allowing people to experience the consequences of the empire's destructive rule. The destruction of one-third of the world in chapters 8-9, and not the whole world, shows God's merciful limitation of the damage in order that people repent. In the final visions, Revelation imagines "a new heaven and a new earth" (21:1) in which God makes all things new. God renews and redeems the world instead of destroying it. That is, the violence does not enact God's revenge— even though some call for it (6:10)—but it shows God's mercy tempering justice.

Another important dimension involves the figure of the "Lamb standing as if it had been slaughtered" (5:6). In the previous verse, one of the elders invites John to "See, the Lion of the tribe of Judah, the Root of David" (5:5). But in a startling juxtaposition, what he actually sees differs greatly from what he is invited to see. In 5:6, the powerful conquering Lion, king of the beasts, turns out to be a "Lamb standing." Rather than causing suffering by exerting great power, the Lamb appears to have suffered at the hands of power. The Lamb depicts Jesus crucified by Rome. Instead of slaughtering, it has been slaughtered, a verb that commonly represents imperial violence in Revelation (6:4, 9). Instead of inflicting damage, it absorbs imperial violence, even to the point of death. The agent of God's purposes has been a victim of imperial violence (crucifixion), but he is not conquered by it. He stands, a reference to Jesus' resurrection, and is in the heavens (his ascension, or vindication by God). God has outpowered and triumphed over Rome, but has done so not with an act of violence but with a powerful act of giving life to one who was broken and killed. God's life-giving way of working is—in part—an alternative to Rome's methods.

This association of the Lamb with God's life-giving purpose transforms the so-called battle scene in 19:17-21. The scene employs the violent fantasy of warfare but qualifies it significantly. While there is a heavenly army, it does not actually fight (19:19-21). And there are different weapons. The Lamb, or in chapter 19, the rider on the white horse (19:11-21), fights not with a literal sword but with "a sharp sword" that "comes from his mouth" (19:15). He is identified as the "Word of God" (19:13), who reveals, communicates, or verbalizes God's purposes into being. He wears a robe stained not with the blood of others but with his own blood given for others (19:13). He captures the beast and his prophet (19:20) and kills the rest with his sword, but it is "the sword that came from his mouth" (19:21). The scene seems to both imitate and employ imperial military violence but also transposes that violence. The exalted Christ accomplishes victory though revealing and persuading words, not military weapons. The inclusion and healing of the nations in the New Jerusalem show the drawing power of God's presence, which the Lamb reveals (21:23-26; 22:3).

Moreover, followers of the Lamb are forbidden to engage the empire with violence. Living in the seven churches of the province of Asia where economic, civic, and religious participation in the empire was woven into the fabric of everyday life, they are to employ the same means of resistance as the Lamb. They negotiate Rome's world by bearing "faithful witness" (1:5), refusing to compromise, and by coming "out from her" (18:4). Their faithfulness will mean social and economic hardship, even suffering martyrdom as the consequence of their nonviolent faithfulness if necessary. These faithful witnesses compose the army of God and the Lamb (ch. 7). They gain victory not by violence, not by causing suffering to others, but by faithfulness and absorbing violence as the Lamb does (7:14-17) while trusting God to complete God's merciful purposes (chs. 19–22). Their martyrdom results from active but nonviolent resistance that refuses to be intimidated by the empire's violence and denies it the power to determine their loyalties.

Such imaginings of violent and cosmic overthrow, transformation, and punishment of Rome sustain, and are sustained among, powerless groups of Jesus' followers. Committed to God's purposes manifested in Jesus, these groups envision the day when their alternative practices and social interactions replace Rome's oppressive system through God's intervention. These imaginings are the hopeful, in-group protests of an alternative community, directed against Rome but not made public or expressed openly to or against Rome. They speak truth *about* power rather than truth *to* power. These visions do, though, undergird practices of direct and open (nonviolent) confrontation, such as refusing to sacrifice to the emperor and withdrawing from economic and social participation in the empire, with imperial officials and with neighbors and fellow guild or artisan group members (18:4).

# 4. How Do Jesus-Believers Relate to Society?

The question of how Jesus-believers are to engage their society is a central one for Revelation, and it continues to be a central one for contemporary readers of Revelation. How do we participate in our world? As we have seen, the churches in the province of Asia were engaged in culture wars. "Jezebel" and her supporters thought there was no problem with Jesus-believers being active participants in their societies, including their eating food offered to idols and honoring images. John was horrified by these practices and wanted Jesus-believers to retreat from their societies and separate themselves from any such compromising activities (18:4). For many contemporary readers of Revelation, especially those who adopt reading strategy 2, discussed in chapter 1, John's approach means ignoring the issues and challenges of the world and waiting to escape from it by the rapture.

This issue of how to relate to society has been an ongoing one for Christian groups across the millennia. Revelation frames this issue in dualistic terms by presenting two contrasting approaches and positions. One approach is that of John's opposition and withdrawal. Another approach is "Jezebel's" embrace of culture and active participation in it as being something good within God's purposes.

Revelation frames the issue starkly in terms of choosing one side or the other. This stark dualism certainly states the issue clearly. Certainly, in some circumstances, either option of greater societal distance or of more societal participation would be an appropriate option. But there are some limitations in framing it in this way.

127

First, it is not clear exactly what John wants when he calls for Jesus-believers to distance themselves from involvement in imperial society. What exactly does he mean when he calls them to "come out of her" (18:4)? How are they to live if they separate themselves from all social and economic participation in their societies because of pervasive idolatry? John warns that this way is difficult and requires faithful endurance, even martyrdom. But he does not lay out a program of specific actions for readers to implement.

Second, the two positions that Revelation presents—namely those of John and Jezebel—are too simple. Interestingly, in reality, both John's and Jezebel's approaches are more complex and hold together some ambiguous elements. For all John's opposition to the Roman Empire, we have seen that in significant ways he also imitates the empire in envisioning God's reign extending over all. For all Jezebel's acceptance of the culture of the cities in the Roman province of Asia, she rejects a fundamental aspect of this society in claiming that idols have no power or significance. That is, along with their significant differences, John and "Jezebel" share some common ground even though they do not recognize it. Their two positions are not pure or simple but hold together some complex dynamics.

However, a third point shows that these two approaches of rejection and accommodation are not the only ways of engaging this issue of how Jesus-believers relate to their societies. One approach sees elements of rejection and accommodation in a constant interplay. A second approach sees a process and partnership whereby God and Christians are at work within society transforming it so that it is more aligned with God's purposes. This approach is hopeful about the world's renewal. Yet a third approach sees places of tension between God's purposes and cultural values and chooses not to reject those tensions but to live in their midst. So revelation and reason, science and faith, the promise of life and its fulfillment, human striving and divine presence, judgment and mercy coexist. Life is lived in those tensions and struggles, often holding them together in faithfulness to God's purposes. The phrase "in the world but not of it" sums up this third approach.

Revelation raises an important question about how Christians live in their cultural contexts. It is a complex issue and one that needs careful thought and discussion. Revelation paints with broad brushstrokes in offering two perspectives. Perhaps the most effective way ahead involves holding the approaches in tension while recognizing and living for God's gracious, transforming, and life-giving purposes for all of God's creation and society.

# 5. Presentation of Women

Revelation wants its readers to choose allegiance to the Lamb rather than to the Beast(s), loyalty to God and not to the Roman Empire. In other words, it wants its readers to follow John and not Jezebel.

It is important to note that Revelation often sets up these choices along gender lines. John's enemy in the churches, especially Thyatira (2:20-23), is the woman teacher and prophetess Jezebel. His rhetoric about her is violent and vicious. He gives her the nickname of one who led Israel astray into idolatry and was condemned by God. He refuses to recognize that God has called her to teach; he says she "calls herself a prophet" (2:20). He refuses to recognize her teaching as legitimate. He charges her with deceiving or "beguiling" the churches. He sexualizes her, describing her ministry in negative sexual terms as "fornication" and "committing adultery." He will throw her on the bed and in an act of murderous rage kill her children.

Revelation uses similar negative terms for Rome and its empire, thereby allying Jezebel with the empire. Rome is also sexualized as a "great whore" who commits fornication and is condemned by God (17:1-5). The language of "whore" and "fornication" comes from the same Greek word. As a "deceiver," Jezebel is allied with three other deceivers, the devil (12:9), the second beast (13:14), and Babylon/Rome (18:23). All four are condemned and destroyed by God. They are subjected to violence. That is, women are presented negatively in representing faithless accommodation and the false, idolatrous Roman Empire. In John's dualistic world, women represent everything that is bad, everything that is contrary to God's purposes, and everything that leads Jesus-believers away from faithfulness to God. Even followers of the Lamb are imaged as "virgins" because they have not "defiled themselves with women" (14:4), probably an image that denotes their nonobservance of idols.

But is that the whole story? Is this negative presentation of women Revelation's only image of women? Is Revelation harmful for women and for men encouraged to think of women in these negative terms? Significantly, women also figure on the other side of John's dualism. In chapter 12, the woman clothed with the sun—variously identified as Eve, Israel, Mary the mother of Jesus, and the church—is able to withstand the devil. She is presented as faithful to God. Likewise, the New Jerusalem, the city that is the arena of God's purposes and presence, is presented in desirable terms as "a bride adorned for her husband" (21:2). These seem to be very positive images of women who are caught up in God's purposes. Yet they are somewhat restricted images. The woman in chapter 12 is faithful, but her description emphasizes her role in being fertile and producing many children (12:17). The New Jerusalem as a bride and "wife of the Lamb" (21:9) is also sexualized in that she is presented as desirable "for her husband" (21:2). That is, even on the positive side of John's ledger, women seem to be presented primarily in terms of sexual function.

Like all religious language, John's images are of course shaped to a significant degree by the society in which he lives. John both imitates and resists these societal structures. His society often—though not totally—privileged men and relegated women to domestic and subordinate roles. John's images reflect both a disparaging and a valuing of women evident in his society as well as in the biblical traditions.

John's images of men are similarly mixed. John of course presents himself as God's spokesperson. God and Jesus are presented in male terms with great power and authority (1:1-8; 19:11-16). But John also presents his opponents as males. He attacks the Balaamites, named after a male prophet, for their faithless idolatry (2:14). And the dragon, "who is called the Devil and Satan," is presented as a male with great power (12:9). That is, males are especially linked with power and authority, sometimes for the good (God, Jesus, John) and sometimes for the bad (the devil, Balaamites). In the end, God the Father outpowers all others.

The challenge for contemporary readers is to understand the

cultural influences shaping these images but to be careful not to appropriate them without careful thought. Revelation's negative images of women that present women in terms of faithlessness, sexual promiscuity, and violence in no way justify such attitudes and practices toward women. John's attack on Jezebel does not disqualify women from leadership in Christian communities. Likewise, Revelation's positive images do not restrict women to domestic roles of marriage and childbirth. Similarly, the images of males in terms of power and rule do not mean that males alone can exercise these roles. Or when the beatitude in 22:7 blesses "the one who keeps the words of the prophecy," it does not apply to men alone as though only men, and not women, can be faithful.

# Conclusion

Revelation requires careful and discerning engagement. These issues—the role of empires in God's purposes, what God is doing in the world, violence, how to engage society, roles of women and men—are five of the fundamental issues for contemporary disciples of Jesus. They raise significant questions about how we read and interpret Scripture and how it might shape our lives to enact God's good, life-giving, and inclusive purposes.

# Study Questions

1. Which of the five sections in the conclusion do you find most interesting or significant? Why?

2. What questions or issues has Revelation raised for you?

3. Should Revelation be left behind?

APPENDIX

# When and for What Circumstances Was Revelation Written?

lues from within Revelation and references to it from other
writings suggest it was probably written in the 90s C.E.,
some sixty or so years after Jesus was crucified.

Some have tried to find clues within Revelation where it seems
to refer to external events that can be dated. Some have suggested,
for example, on the basis of the depiction, in chapter 11, of an
attack on Jerusalem in which the Temple is not destroyed that
Revelation must have been written before the destruction of the
Jerusalem Temple by the Romans in 70 C.E. But this conclusion is
not certain since the author of Revelation could have imagined all
sorts of things. For example, in 13:2 he imagines a beast that combines features of a leopard, a bear, and a lion.

Others have tried to draw conclusions about when it was written from the reference to kings in 17:9-11:

> The seven heads are seven mountains on which the woman is seated;
> also, they are seven kings, of whom five have fallen, one is living,
> and the other has not yet come; and when he comes, he must
> remain only a little while. As for the beast that was and is not, it is
> an eighth but it belongs to the seven, and it goes to destruction.

Assuming that these kings are emperors (and there is some
debate), the key phrase is the reference in verse 10 to five who

have "fallen" (Augustus, Tiberius, Caligula, Claudius, Nero) and to "one is living." Who is this sixth emperor? The problem is whether or not to count the three emperors Galba, Otho, and Vitellius, who ruled for just a matter of months each in the chaotic years 68 and 69. If we do so, the inconsequential Galba is the sixth and Revelation was written in 68 C.E. But if we skip over these relatively insignificant and short-lived emperors in favor of the next long-serving emperor, Vespasian, who ruled from 69 through 79, we would consider him the sixth. Those who choose the second option understand Revelation to have been written sometime in the 70s.

Others find some confirmation for this claim by noting the way that Revelation looks back especially on the reign of the emperor Nero, who died in 68. There were legends circulating that Nero was returning to Rome, either from the dead or from exile (on the basis that he hadn't died in 68). Such legends are well attested in the early second century in writers such as Suetonius (*Nero* 57) and Tacitus (*Histories* 2.8-9).

Also relevant here is the number "666" that appears in 13:18. This is the number of "the beast," the paradigmatic evil figure who opposes God's purposes. Languages like Hebrew and Latin could use letters with numerical values as a means of counting. The numerical value of the name "Nero Caesar" in Hebrew adds up to six hundred sixty-six. If this is a correct identification (and finally, that is not certain), it shows Revelation looking back on the emperor Nero as the epitome of evil. To do so, Revelation would have to have been written sometime (how much time?) after Nero's death in 68 C.E.

From these various links with Nero (the fifth emperor), we might posit a time span from 68 to about 110 as a possible time span within which Revelation was written.

The other means of dating Revelation is to draw on evidence from writers who attest its existence. For example, Justin Martyr wrote a lengthy work called *Dialogue with Trypho* in the early to mid-second century in which he summarized some of the content of Revelation:

> And further, there was a certain man with us, whose name was John, one of the apostles of Christ, who prophesied, by a revelation that was made to him, that those who believed in our Christ would

dwell a thousand years in Jerusalem; and that thereafter the general, and, in short, the eternal resurrection and judgment of all people would likewise take place. (*Dialogue with Trypho* 81.4)

This summary of aspects of Revelation indicates that by the early to mid-second century, the book of Revelation had to have been in existence.

Later in the second century, the writer Irenaeus offered some further evidence for this time period. Irenaeus had been discussing the number of the beast (666) that Revelation used in 13:18. Irenaeus said he could not identify who this figure was

"for if it were necessary that his name should be distinctly revealed in this present time, it would have been announced by him who beheld the apocalyptic vision. For that was seen no very long time since, but almost in our day, towards the end of Domitian's reign." (*Against Heresies* 5.30.3)

Irenaeus linked the writing of Revelation to being "towards the end of Domitian's reign." Domitian was emperor, the eighth or eleventh emperor, from 81 through 96 C.E. "Towards the end of Domitian's reign" would put the writing of Revelation in the 90s. Irenaeus did not indicate how he knew this information, so we can't evaluate its reliability.

We cannot, then, be certain as to the exact year when Revelation was written, but from the few clues that we have, we can establish a reasonable window of opportunity from the 70s to around 100 C.E.

## Revelation and Persecution?

As important as the likely date, though, is the question of the circumstances that prompted the writing of this book. On the basis of the seven letters in chapters 2–3 (discussed in this book in chapters 3–4), Revelation was addressed to Christians living in cities in the area that we know today as Turkey but which in the first century was known as the Roman province of Asia. These Christians, so it is often (but erroneously) claimed, were being persecuted for their faith by the Roman Empire, especially the emperor

Domitian. Those who construct this scenario point to references to persecution in Revelation such as:

- warnings about persecution: "Do not fear what you are about to suffer. Beware, the devil is about to throw some of you into prison" (2:10).
- Antipas the martyr: "you did not deny your faith in me even in the days of Antipas my witness, my faithful one, who was killed among you, where Satan lives" (2:13).
- other martyrs in visionary scenes: "I saw under the altar the souls of those who had been slaughtered for the word of God and for the testimony they had given," (6:9) including the ghastly image of the woman who represents Rome who is "drunk with the blood of the saints and the blood of the witnesses to Jesus" (17:6).

Those who think persecution comprises the circumstances that Revelation addresses argue that the persecution came about because the emperor Domitian had demanded that he be worshiped as "Lord and God" in the imperial cult. A new temple, for example, was dedicated for the worship of the emperors in Ephesus in 88–89.

What are we to make of this scenario of persecution? While it picks up some elements of Revelation, it is finally not convincing or adequate for making sense of the writing.

- We should note that references to persecution like 2:10 locate the persecution in the future. Revelation imagines a future persecution rather than addressing a present context marked by persecution. The references in the worship scenes to martyrs (6:9-11; 7:14; 16:6; 18:24) similarly indicate those who will suffer and "come out of the great ordeal" that is yet to take place (7:14).
- And the reference in 2:13 to Antipas the martyr? He is the only actual martyr presented in Revelation. And he is located sometime in the past, "even in the days of Antipas."
- Further, there is no evidence that Rome or the emperor Domitian instigated persecution of Christians in the late first

century. There was no law requiring that everybody worship, or offer sacrifice to, the emperor. There was no empire-wide, empire-initiated persecution of Christians until the emperor Decius initiated persecution against Christians in the mid-third century. There were, though, isolated outbreaks of persecution. Around the year 64, after the fire of Rome, the emperor Nero had persecuted some Christians in Rome, though his reason for doing so is not clear. There is no evidence that Nero's actions had anything to do with worshiping the emperor or even making Christian confession. It was a short-lived persecution. It was not sustained over a period of time, and it was definitely not extended over the whole empire. There is also some evidence that there were local conflicts between Christians and their neighbors. This perhaps explains the isolated reference to Antipas (2:13).

Most Christians, though, probably lived peaceably in towns and cities throughout the empire. It is this situation of active participation in their civic contexts that gives rise to the central issue that I highlight in this book: how were Jesus-believers to negotiate their interactions with their societies, in which observance of idols pervaded almost every aspect of daily life, yet remain faithful to their commitment to follow Jesus?

CPSIA information can be obtained
at www.ICGtesting.com
Printed in the USA
FSOW02n1755080118
43179FS